3/09

D1193447

ST. LOUIS POST-DISPATCH

BOOKS

Bernie's Best

FAVORITE SPORTS COLUMNS BY BERNIE MIKLASZ OF THE ST. LOUIS POST-DISPATCH

FOREWORD BY BOB COSTAS

ST. LOUIS POST-DISPATCH
BOOKS

EDITOR
Mike Smith

ART DIRECTOR & DESIGNER
Wade Wilson

PHOTO EDITOR
Larry Coyne

WRITER
Bernie Miklasz

CONTRIBUTING WRITER
Bob Costas

ASSISTANT PHOTO EDITOR
Hillary Levin

SALES & MARKETING
Tracy Rouch

Special thanks to Doug Weaver of Kansas City Star Books

Softcover
ISBN 978-0-9796054-3-7

Printed by Walsworth Publishing Co., Marceline, Mo.

To order additional copies, call 1-800-329-0224
Order online at www.post-dispatchstore.com

CONTENTS

Columns appear as originally published by the Post-Dispatch, with some edited for length. Each "Bernie Bit" is his reminiscence about the topic. All photo captions are excerpts from Bernie's columns. Dates on the columns are Post-Dispatch publication dates.

ABOUT BERNIE

Bernie Miklasz is a Baltimore native, and though he still counts John Unitas and Brooks Robinson among his sports heroes, he is a full-fledged St. Louisan, too. Ask him where he was educated, and he tells you where he went to high school (Archbishop Spalding in Baltimore).

Miklasz — as he says, it's pronounced "just like Jack Nicklaus, but with an M" — has been a St. Louis Post-Dispatch sports columnist since 1989, but his reach extends well beyond the newspaper's audience. He hosts a popular online forum for fans — Bernie's Press Box on STLtoday.com, the website for the Post-Dispatch. He also authors a blog, Bernie's Extra Points, for the site; co-hosts an afternoon sports-talk radio show in St. Louis; and is a regular contributor on the Fox Sports Network.

Miklasz covered high school sports for the Arundel (Md.) Observer and the Annapolis (Md.) Evening Capital before the Baltimore News American hired him in 1979. Name a sport, and he probably wrote about it for the News American, which promoted him to beat writer for the Colts and Redskins and then to columnist.

In 1985, the Post-Dispatch hired Miklasz to cover the football Cardinals, a job for which he would prove to be uniquely qualified. Just as the Colts had fled Baltimore for Indianapolis when he covered them, the Big Red left St. Louis for Arizona in 1988. Miklasz left, too, jumping to the Dallas Morning News to cover the Cowboys. But he soon returned when the Post-Dispatch — about to face off against a new tabloid in a St. Louis "newspaper war" — hired him to be its sports columnist.

For almost two decades, Miklasz has been an authoritative voice on sports in St. Louis. Miklasz has written about the Cardinals in two World Series, the Rams in two Super Bowls, the Olympics on three continents, the Final Four in St. Louis and around the U.S., Michael Jordan in the NBA Finals, and much more. He is one of 44 selectors for the Pro Football Hall of Fame and also votes annually in the Baseball Hall of Fame, Heisman Trophy and NL Cy Young Award balloting.

FOREWORD

BY BOB COSTAS

On Sept. 27, 1953, the Browns played their last baseball game in St. Louis. Inexplicably turning their backs on throngs of supporters averaging just under 4,000 per game, the Browns absconded to Baltimore, where they became the Orioles. The move paid immediate dividends.

The Browns had made their last stand with a record of 54-100. The new-look Orioles improved on that by going 55-99. So who can argue with success? Of course, before long Brooks Robinson would turn up, and eventually Jim Palmer, Boog Powell, Frank Robinson and a bunch of other guys who actually could play. So, the Orioles of the 1960s and '70s (managed by St. Louisan Earl Weaver) became one of baseball's great teams.

And what did we have to show for it? I mean, just to get them started, St. Louis gave the Baltimore Orioles Don Larsen, Clint Courtney, Vern Stephens and Vic Wertz, not to mention Billy Hunter, Don Lenhardt, Bob Turley and Lou Kretlow. And what does St. Louis get out of the deal? I'll tell you what — ever more distant memories of one-armed outfielder Pete Gray and the pinch-hit walk drawn in 1951 by 3-foot-7 Eddie Gaedel. Where, I ask you, is the equity? Which brings us — sort of — to my point.

In the mid-1980s, the fair city of Baltimore finally came to terms with its guilt and attempted to make amends. As at least partial payment for the services of the remarkably consistent second baseman Bobby Young (4 homers, 25 RBIs for the '53 Browns; 4 and 24 for the '54 O's), the Charm City sent a promising prospect our way. Bernie Miklasz, Baltimore born and bred, had gotten some seasoning at a minor league outpost called the Baltimore News American. Now he would try his hand in the big leagues, first as the NFL writer and then as the lead sports columnist for the St. Louis Post-Dispatch. Almost 20 years later, Bernie is still writing columns. That, by the way, is a longer St. Louis tenure than *any* Brownie, and while it doesn't approach Broeg or Burnes territory, it's still an impressive run, observing and chronicling St. Louis sports.

Now, at this point, I could say something like, "I consider Bernie the greatest literary talent to come out of Baltimore since Edgar Allan Poe." But why resort to the obvious? Instead, here's what I like about Bernie's work: It's clear he has a St. Louis perspective, but he combines it with a national perspective. He wants the local teams to do well, but his broader view allows for context and measured judgment. As any good columnist must, he has strong viewpoints, but unlike many in his profession, Bernie feels an obligation to actually make a convincing case, so he presents informed and coherent arguments to back up his opinions.

At a time when potshots and invective rule talk radio and the Internet, and sadly have seeped into the mainstream media as well, Bernie still respects his subject matter and his readership enough to make consistently strong but thoughtful points. He knows the difference between a critique and a cheap shot. Between being tough and being mean-spirited.

No sports fan could ever doubt that Bernie is one of us. His writing often captures the pure joy and drama of a great game but also the disillusionment and disappointment we all feel at times. Bernie genuinely loves his job — turning up at more games, events and practices than there are days on the calendar. He is constantly seeking and absorbing information. That kind of legwork is reflected in his columns. Talent and craft are always appreciated. But part of being a good newspaperman is working sources and wearing out the shoe leather. It's one thing to criticize a player, manager or general manager. It's another to show up in the dugout, locker room or front office the next day and take the heat that sometimes comes with the territory. Like the best of his colleagues, Bernie has made a career out of that.

I hope his readers understand and appreciate that kind of professionalism. The point is not that any of us should agree with Bernie all the time. I know I don't — but I have always respected the honest effort, professional skill and accumulated insight he brings to the Post-Dispatch.

After almost 20 years in St. Louis, Bernie Miklasz is still a must read. Here now, some of the best from a memorable two decades spent at the heart of St. Louis sports.

St. Louis sports fans remember Bob Costas as the basketball play-by-play voice of the old Spirits of St. Louis and the Missouri Tigers in the 1970s. Millions of Americans currently know him as the prime-time host for NBC's coverage of the Olympics and the NFL, and as host of "Costas Now" on HBO.

INTRODUCTION

BY BERNIE MIKLASZ

When I was offered a chance to return to St. Louis and the Post-Dispatch in the summer of 1989, I jumped at it. Sure, I was motivated by the opportunity to write a column, which was a career goal. But I missed St. Louis and wanted to come back.

I'd left the paper to go to the Dallas Morning News after being offered the Cowboys beat. It isn't that I wanted to leave St. Louis, but at that stage of my career, I was a football writer and loved covering the beat, and I wasn't ready to give that up. The Cardinals had moved to Arizona, and I had no team to cover.

So I made the decision to go. And, yeah, I did feel disloyal to an extent. As I was driving away, on the road to Dallas, I was filled with sadness. But I'll admit it: Career ambition carried the day.

And when the Dallas Morning News asks you to take over the paper's No. 1 beat, it's a job that you just can't turn down. But I sincerely missed living in St. Louis. So when the Post-Dispatch graciously extended an offer to return as a columnist, I barked out "Yes!" before anyone there could change their mind.

Given a second chance, I didn't want to betray the newspaper's loyalty, or the city's loyalty, to me. And as I settled in as a columnist, I always tried to keep this principle in mind: It was never up to St. Louis to adapt to me; it was up to me to adjust to St. Louis. It was my responsibility to get in tune with the city, and the readers, and to tap into the history and the tradition and the endearing quirkiness that make this such a charming place.

I wanted to prove myself worthy of this opportunity. It sounds corny, but I am really grateful for all that St. Louis has done for me. In the late 1970s, if you had told me that I'd rise to the level of writing a high-profile column in a town that I love, a town that is crazy about sports, a town that would accept me so warmly, I would have considered that a dream, a fantasy.

Accordingly, I never forget about my humble origins. Growing up in Baltimore, I was a restless kid who didn't have much money for college, and I had to scratch out a career by working harder and being more resourceful than the college-trained journalists who entered the industry with a superior education and credentials.

My first newspaper job, at the Baltimore News American, paid minimum wage. But I was thrilled to answer the phones, make coffee, run the horse racing results to the composing room, or assist veteran reporters at crime scenes in the middle of the night. I made myself useful in every way and was willing to work around the clock. It was a berserk but exciting way to live.

At age 19 or thereabouts, I begged the editors to give me a chance to write a story. My opening came when another writer called in sick and there was no one available to cover the last appearance in Washington, D.C., of retiring hockey immortal Gordie Howe. The boss warned me: Kid, if you turn in the copy and it stinks, we won't run it. So make it good.

I submitted the Howe story, and the newspaper published it.

Many more stories followed.

Figures that the first one would be about a hockey player. I considered myself a grinder then, and a grinder now.

I may have disappointed readers with some of my opinions through the years, and as a younger columnist I was awfully petulant at times. But I hope that the readers realize I've never cheated them with my effort. For whatever it's worth, I still feel as if I owe St. Louis and the Post-Dispatch a huge debt of gratitude for giving me a wonderful home, a privileged platform and that fantasy career. I can't thank you enough. All I can do is keep grinding.

"If you had told me that I'd rise to the level of writing a high-profile column in a town that I love, a town that is crazy about sports ... I would have considered that a dream, a fantasy."

"At 10:22 on the evening of Oct. 27, 2006, rookie Cardinals closer Adam Wainwright struck out the Tigers' Brandon Inge on a heinous breaking ball, sealing the 10th World Series championship in Cardinals history."

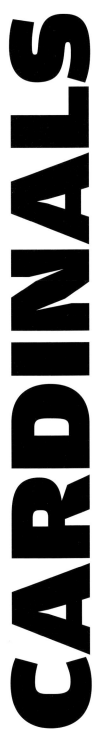

It's hard to say goodbye to a Jim-dandy center fielder

BERNIE BIT • Of all the Cardinals I've covered, Jim Edmonds was the most entertaining in every way. He produced dramas on the field, and drama off the field. He had the cynical, jaded, twisted wit that one usually associates with a sportswriter, which is why I probably liked him so much.

We're going to miss the ballet in center field, the Jimnastics, the swan dives for the baseball. We'll miss the way he'd jump to his feet to proudly display the grass stains and the dirt that were smeared across his uniform.

We'll miss the theater, and his actor's sense of timing as he tracked that elusive fly ball. The way he envisioned and marked the landing spot ahead of time, knowing just how far he had to go, and arriving just in time to deliver that extra suspense, that extra drama. All of the web gems, the web Jims, he created.

And after crashing to the turf, or into a wall, he'd milk the moment by immediately sinking to his knees, roll over and writhe in pain, going down as if he had just been smacked on the forehead by a wrecking ball. Miraculously, he would rise, and slowly trot back to the Cardinals' dugout, taking a little extra time to let the applause wash over him and heal his bruises, his psyche.

And then there was the swing: so fluid and sweet and so smooth that it did not disturb the summer breeze.

And the mood swings were almost as fun.

It was all so very entertaining: his good–natured heckling of the unwashed press corps; his self–deprecating style; his crabbiness on a hot day at the ballpark after a short night; and the compelling psychodrama of a relationship he had with his stern manager, Tony La Russa.

Jim Edmonds was the good boy, the bad boy.

Most of all, he was the boy of summer who would never grow old.

Sadly, Edmonds did wear down. After averaging 34 homers and 96 RBIs in his first six seasons as a Cardinal, Edmonds' productivity the last two seasons dropped to a rate of 14 homers and 55 RBIs.

After running down all of those line drives in the gaps, he couldn't outrun his age. He'll be 38 next season, and hopes to kick–start his career back home in SoCal.

"Jimmy's flamboyant way of getting it done in crucial ways came through many times, especially in the 2004 NLCS. There was the winning homer in Game 6, and the saving catch in Game 7. The kind of stuff that gives you chills."

Jimmy Baseball has gone away.

"The friendships will last forever," Edmonds said. "And I'll always cherish those friendships. And I will never lose them."

The Cardinals agreed to his request for a trade, so Edmonds is off to join the San Diego Padres. In return the Cardinals get David Freese, a strapping third-base prospect who grew up in St. Louis, cheering for Edmonds, just like most folks.

As he departs, how do we frame Edmonds' career?

If we consider the combination of offense and defense, Edmonds was the best overall center fielder in Cardinals history.

That's no hype or phony, parting-gift praise.

Edmonds played eight seasons here. And among all hitters in franchise history he ranks fourth in homers, 12th in RBIs, and sixth in combined on base-slugging percentage. No other Cardinals center fielder comes close to matching the wattage of that offensive production, and Edmonds won six Gold Gloves in eight St. Louis summers.

Jimmy's flamboyant way of getting it done in crucial ways came through many times, especially in the 2004 National League Championship Series against Houston. There was the winning homer in Game 6, and the saving catch in Game 7. The kind of stuff that gives you chills.

Edmonds was the all-around performer who gave us an extended thrill ride after arriving unexpectedly from the Angels in the spring of 2000.

Edmonds played a leading role in transforming this franchise, fueling the Cardinals' offense and defense with an abundance of natural talent.

The baseball gods gave Jimmy a gift, and he shared it with the Cardinals and their fans. It's the end of a dazzling era.

McGwire casts long shadow over Hall of Fame weekend

BERNIE BIT • It's almost as if Mark McGwire's career never happened. It's almost as if he'd erased himself from the record books, and from our memories, on that fateful day on Capitol Hill, when he told Congress that he wasn't there to talk about the past. It's sad.

COOPERSTOWN, N.Y.

This was supposed to be a table reserved for three: Tony Gwynn, Cal Ripken and Mark McGwire.

It would be one of the most renowned Hall of Fame induction classes in the history of the shrine. Here was Gwynn, the master baseball violinist, killing pitchers softly with his 3,141 base hits. And the great Ripken, the iron man who changed the game by bringing a hammer of offensive power to the shortstop position. And McGwire, he of the mighty strength and prodigious home runs.

Only Gwynn and Ripken are here.

How did this happen?

In some ways, it's incomprehensible. Think back to 1998, when McGwire slammed a record 70 home runs to re–energize a sport, thrill the nation and give even the most abandoned of stadiums a full house and the feel of a sold–out rock-and-roll show.

Think back to when McGwire was named Time magazine's "Man of the Year" for 1998, prompting Daniel Okrent to write: "We needed Mark McGwire in 1998, needed him desperately."

Nearly 10 years later, McGwire is but a ghost. He is out there somewhere, hanging over the game's recent history but rarely seen, and the mere mention of his name evokes howling. The cobwebs are forming on his career line of 583 homers, and the doors to the Baseball Hall of Fame will probably remain sealed off to him forever.

As baseball's steroids scandal blew up, McGwire was the first test case for Hall of Fame voters, the first suspected juicer to be rounded up and placed before a jury of baseball writers. And the writers affixed the scarlet letter ("S") to his name. McGwire was given only 25 percent of the necessary 75 votes for passage into Cooperstown. The rejection was adamant. The message couldn't be clearer.

Gwynn and Ripken, meanwhile, received 98 percent of the vote. They are being venerated as baseball saints, and two good guys who personify all that is pure and natural about a game that Americans want to idealize. Gwynn and Ripken are the perfect goodwill ambassadors to counteract the freak show on the other side of the continent, by the bay in San Francisco.

It is safe to love Ripken and Gwynn, safe to travel through the rolling hills and pristine meadows of rural upstate New York to find the field of gold, the field of dreams, that will serve as the stage for their awaited induction.

"Of all the bad things going in sports today, those guys are two of the good things," Cardinals Hall of Famer Ozzie Smith said. "This is a nice break from all the negative things going on. You look at those two guys and it would be very hard to find two better representatives of what the game is about."

That's the unofficial theme here this weekend: It is safe to come home again, to believe in the authenticity of baseball heroes ...

At least until Barry Bonds pierces the soul of baseball by launching home run No. 756.

Gwynn and Ripken are so gloriously happy, it got me to thinking about McGwire. What is he feeling? Is he sad? Mad at the game that turned on him? Does he regret any of his choices? Does he care at all? Does the Hall of Fame mean anything to him, does he even want to be a member? McGwire is silent, so we have no idea.

As for possible enshrinement in the future, I don't see a way in for McGwire, or a way out of this mess. By refusing to deny steroid use or own up to it in his testimony before a congressional subcommittee on March 17, 2005, McGwire immolated his Hall of Fame chances.

McGwire has declined to defend his reputation or rehabilitate his name. Rather than publicly campaign, he'd rather play golf and enjoy his private life with his wife and two children.

Even if McGwire comes clean or does the opposite and swears under oath that he never did steroids, I don't think it matters. When he retired after the 2001 season with 583 homers, Mac was one of only 17 men with 500-plus homers. By the end of 2008, that list will probably be at 25. In retirement, McGwire's 583 already has been exceeded by Bonds, Ken Griffey Jr. and Sammy Sosa. And there's a long line of sluggers progressing toward 500, and 583, and they will zoom by McGwire's historical marker.

Big Mac's 583 homers will be substantially devalued. And if McGwire ever decides (if at all) to plead his case for Cooperstown, it'll probably be too late. McGwire is destined to travel alone into baseball history as the unforgotten, but unforgiven.

World Series title puts painful memories to rest

BERNIE BIT • I remember walking into the chilly autumn night a few hours after Adam Wainwright ended it with a strikeout, and seeing so many happy Cardinals fans, who just couldn't bring themselves to go home. They just wanted to be with each other, deep into the wee small hours, to share the experience and keep that glorious moment alive for as long as they could.

The 10th World Series championship in Cardinals history was for all the Cardinals teams of the past that played special baseball all summer, only to come up short, staggering off into the winter, filled with frustration and longing.

This was to give peace to all of the postseason ghosts and to soften the haunted memories, whether it's Curt Flood's slip in 1968, or umpire Don Denkinger's blown call at first base in 1985, or the hydraulic tarp that swallowed Vince Coleman's ankle.

This was for the franchise immortals who always return home, a college of Cardinals, visiting this baseball Vatican in St. Louis. They are living monuments: Stan Musial, Bob Gibson, Lou Brock, Ozzie Smith, Red Schoendienst and Bruce Sutter. Their presence reminds new generations of Cardinals that theirs is an extraordinary legacy, always to be handled with care.

This was for old friends who could not be there, but you just know that the spirits of Jack Buck and Darryl Kile were close to the Cardinals and their fans, watching over the drama of Game 5.

This was for baseball's best fans, who had waited 23 seasons for a reaffirmation of the proud franchise's glorious tradition. It doesn't matter where they were gathered for Game 5. They could have been shivering in the frigid bowl of Busch Stadium, or watching by the fireplace at home, or bonding with friends in a local sports bar, or watching on satellite from a base camp in Iraq, or an outpost in Afghanistan.

Cardinals fans live everywhere, existing as one extended family, and they became one nation under a groove again on Friday night, when the power of this Red October pulled their heartbeats together in an electric moment. At 10:22 on the evening of Oct. 27, 2006, rookie Cardinals closer Adam Wainwright struck out the Tigers' Brandon

"No one in a Cardinals uniform has ever worked harder or cared more deeply or lost more sleep in the quest of a World Series championship. And on this night, La Russa finally became a champ again."

Inge on a heinous breaking ball, sealing World Series title No. 10 with a 4-2 victory in Game 5.

"We shocked the world," Cardinals center fielder Jim Edmonds said on the field, moments after the game.

Their summer of lurching to 83 wins was traded in for a month of unexpected excellence. Their season of agony was exchanged for October ecstasy. Six months of adversity and trouble was washed away by champagne and bubbles in a postgame house party.

One man stood in the center of it all, nearly incapable of comprehending the magnitude of the scene.

"I'm having a hard time holding it together," manager Tony La Russa said.

This championship was for La Russa, too. When he accepted the Cardinals job after the 1995 season, he specifically asked for No. 10. More than a number, it represented an ideal, a goal, a mission statement. The Cardinals had won the World Series nine times, and La Russa wanted to collect the 10th for the franchise.

"As soon as you put the uniform on," La Russa said, "you realize it comes with an attachment. There's a special pressure and responsibility. And that's good. It really drives you."

At times the No. 10 got awfully heavy, as the intense La Russa worked himself into a high level of stress. He'd get close, only to be denied again, and demonized again. La Russa absorbed criticism, stirred controversy and had the name "Whitey Herzog" thrown in his face a million times.

La Russa did it his way, and whether you like him or not, this is the absolute truth: No one in a Cardinals uniform has ever worked harder or cared more deeply or lost more sleep in the quest of a World Series championship. And on this night, La Russa finally became a champ again.

"Winning a World Series is always special," La Russa said. "But we had so many opportunities here. It's been 11 years. So this is something that you really cherish."

La Russa's small office was packed. His wife Elaine was there; earlier they'd hugged and kissed near the Cardinals dugout only seconds after Wainwright finished what Jeff Weaver started to make 46,638 hearts skip at Busch.

An hour later, La Russa's pulse was still racing. This was his seventh postseason team in St. Louis. And who would have imagined this assortment of bruised players, slumping stars, limping veterans, precocious kids, recycled parts and superstars Albert Pujols and Chris Carpenter would rally, unify, and pull off a miracle? La Russa is only the second manager in baseball history to win a World Series in both leagues, and that distinction will guarantee his spot in Cooperstown.

In late September, did you see this coming?

"I'm not that optimistic," Elaine La Russa said. "I'm a realist. And a lot of bad stuff came down this year."

In the end, these flawed but resilient Cardinals did it for superior St. Louis teams that didn't survive October. The Cardinals' postseason universe was balanced in this fantasy October.

When La Russa saw Bob Gibson after Game 5, the meaning of it all suddenly rushed through his blood.

"When you're here," La Russa said, "you can't join the club unless you win the World Series. And now we can say this group joined the club."

In his 1,851st game as the Cardinals manager, regular season and postseason, Tony La Russa got it done. The number on his back is no longer 10 pounds of burdensome weight, or the symbol of an unfulfilled promise. It stands for 10 World Series championships.

An imperfect team delivered a perfect 10.

Season of torment stays tough to the end

BERNIE BIT • By winning so dramatically, the Cardinals all but caused a citywide power blackout in NYC. Except for the Mike Jones tackle that preserved the Rams' victory in Super Bowl 34, it was the most stunning happy ending I'd witnessed from a press box. The problem is, I had about 20 minutes to write this column and make sense of it all. I killed some brain cells that night at Shea.

NEW YORK

It was never easy for the 2006 Cardinals, not for one day. It was a season of torment, from the injuries, to the losing streaks, to the controversies, to the late-season crisis of confidence that nearly wiped them out.

So you knew it would come down to this, a fight and a struggle to the very end of the National League Championship Series. The Cardiac Cardinals would leave every heart in the place on the ground, leave our lungs short of oxygen, pull on the emotions of two cities and make every suspenseful pitch feel like a sharp jab to the ribs.

In a remarkable and simply amazing Game 7 of the NLCS, the raging drama never was cooled until the last pitch. Not even by the mist that drizzled over the playing field at raucous Shea Stadium, a hint of the hard rain that soon would fall to douse the Mets and their fans. The Mets and Cardinals locked into a memorable, mind-bending duel that exhausted anyone who saw it.

"It had to be one of the best baseball games ever played," rookie Cardinals closer Adam Wainwright said. "Just unbelievable tension right to the last pitch."

There was Cardinals starter Jeff Suppan, who pitched from his heart for seven wondrous innings, battling and bottling the Mets' renowned bats to a 1-1 draw in a performance that defined his career as a supreme competitor.

There was Mets left fielder Endy Chavez, who made the catch of a lifetime, stealing a two-run homer from Scott Rolen in the sixth inning, threatening to bury the Cardinals' dreams in the webbing of his glove.

And in a season with so many crazy twists, and in a Game 7 that tested the nerves of the most calloused athletes, it would be up to a couple of players to capture the night by being a little stronger and tougher than all the rest.

So when fate clicked into motion and turned to finally decide Game

"Bulldog catcher Yadier Molina, who carried the weakest bat in the lineup all year ... gunned a two-run homer over the wall. 'It was,' Molina said, 'the best moment of my life.' "

7, we shouldn't have been surprised by what happened, or who did it. Because if we've learned anything this season, it's this: There is nothing normal about these St. Louis Cardinals. Not the 83 wins in the regular season, not the relentless summer strife, and not this October rising.

And so it came to pass in the top of the ninth that Rolen, the previous victim, fought his way to a single off Mets reliever Aaron Heilman. And so it came to pass that next up was bulldog catcher Yadier Molina, who carried the weakest bat in the lineup all year. He's had a good October, though, and manager Tony La Russa moved Molina up a spot in the batting order for Game 7. A premonition, perhaps?

And so it came to pass that Molina took his .216 stick and gunned a two-run homer over the wall in left for a 3-1 lead.

"It was," Molina said, "the best moment of my life."

And so it came to pass in the bottom of the ninth that Wainwright, the inexperienced rookie closer, worked himself into a heap of trouble. The bases were loaded with two out and 56,357 howling wolves baying at him from the Shea galleries.

And now, the tipping point ...

When Wainwright threw a perfect curve to freeze Cardinals killer Carlos Beltran for a called third strike, Molina squeezed it hard.

The clock at Shea Stadium read 11:44 p.m.

Remember the Simon and Garfunkel hit, "Sounds of Silence"?

Well, Molina was Simon.

Wainwright was Garfunkel.

Because someone pressed a mute button at Shea, and it seemed like nothing could be heard except the noise being generated by shouting, jumping, jubilant Cardinals.

The Cardinals had a 3-1 victory. It was over, just like that, the drama and the Mets' season. The Cardinals made true believers out of the skeptics who said it couldn't be done.

An 83-win team, going to the World Series?

Can't happen.

Impossible.

But that victory celebration on the green at Shea was confirmation: The Cardinals are indeed heading to Detroit for the 2006 World Series.

"It's an indescribable feeling," said lefty reliever Randy Flores, who got the win.

Red October still is going strong.

Chavez tried to ruin it all by taking a two-run homer away from Rolen in the sixth. ... Still, the Cardinals had Suppan, their own line of defense. And Suppan was nothing short of heroic in this Game 7, holding the Mets hitless from the end of the first inning until he walked off the mound in the bottom of the eighth.

Suppan pressed on through the night, unfazed by the powerful Mets and the cacophony at Shea. Suppan was a one-man buzz kill, especially in the bottom of the sixth when he wiggled out of a bases-loaded predicament, a few minutes after Chavez had pumped up the place with the big grab.

Suppan's greatest effort wasn't wasted. When Molina pounced on Heilman's high changeup, he sent it a long way, to a place where Chavez couldn't go. All the way to Comerica Park in Detroit, to Game 1 of the World Series.

04.10.2006

The new ballpark: an urban paradise for Cardinals fans

BERNIE BIT • I don't know how the "new" Busch Stadium will hold up, or how we'll feel about it 40 or 50 years from now, but there is always something tremendously exciting when a ballpark opens. On that first day, the possibilities for the future are endless. We're just waiting for the history to be filled in.

In "Take Time For Paradise," his eloquent book of essays, the late baseball commissioner Bart Giamatti explored the soulful, soothing appeal of the games that appeal to us.

"Sports," Giamatti wrote, "represent a shared vision of how we continue, as individual, team or community, to experience a happiness or absence of care so intense, so rare, and so fleeting that we associate their experience with experience otherwise described as religious."

And at the heart of this longing is the great American ballpark. To Giamatti, a day at a beautiful ballpark was as pleasurable as an imagined visit to the garden of Eden.

"The word 'paradise' is originally an old Persian word meaning an enclosed park or green," Giamatti once explained in an interview. "Anything that's closed is fundamentally artificial. Nature doesn't enclose things perfectly. You fly over a great city at night and you look down and you see lit up this green in the middle of the city and you realize that the reason they're in the middle of cities is that there is in us a fundamental, vestigial memory of an enclosed green space as the place of freedom or play."

Yes, and a trip to the ballpark is also great fun — whether it's keeping score, second-guessing the manager, buying something new and red from the souvenir stand, snacking on favorite treats, sipping on a cold beer, leaning back to bask in the sun or having a pleasant conversation with the friend, loved one or total stranger in the seat next to you.

When new stadium gates swing open, it's an extraordinary awakening. I can't speak from personal experience, but in some way it must have felt like this on all the Opening Days of St. Louis past. At Grand Avenue Grounds, Union Park, League Park, Robison Field, Sportsman's Park, and the Busch Stadium that closed on Oct. 19, 2005. (Thanks for nothing, Roy Oswalt.)

It's time to usher in a new era. It's a shame that Giamatti, who truly treasured the game, can't be in downtown St. Louis today to savor the official opening of our grand new ballpark. But more than 40,000 will come together today. Our celebrated baseball community will reunite, renew. Baseball's best fans have a new playground, and this should be one of the most special and memorable days in our city's history.

Sure, there will be confusion, and a mild state of disorientation. There may even be chaos, which is to be expected when 40,000-plus parade into a new space to sort everything out. If you've ever moved into a new home, you know that it usually takes weeks to get to know every inch of the place, and settle into familiar patterns and rhythms. The new residence is your formal address from the first day you move in, but it takes time to truly become your home.

So today at Busch Stadium there will likely be long lines, hesitation and uncertainty during the attempt to match tickets to seat locations. There will be a search for that preferred hot dog, a test run to determine how many at-bats you'll miss during a stop at the restroom. At moments the experience could border on overwhelming.

It's OK. It's your new baseball home, and you will love it, even if it will take several tours to discover all there is to know. Heck, the place isn't entirely finished yet. Parts of the left-field area are still under construction. And the full ambiance won't be realized until the planned Ballpark Village begins to form around the perimeter.

And that's fine, too. It was that way at the previous Busch Stadium. On the first day — May 12, 1966 — legendary sportswriter Red Smith wrote: "Even as the customers arrived, muscular men were toting bottled goods into the elegant Stadium Club, laying tile, setting up paneling, clearing debris and tussling with the mechanical tarpaulin roller that had refused to work."

The unfinished pieces only create more anticipation; it's as if this Opening Day will be stretched out over days, months and years. It will be exciting to watch the new Busch breathe, evolve, grow, take root, form a personality, gradually mature, cultivate a unique ambiance and stand invincibly and impressively as the familiar centerpiece of our baseball lives.

In time, the first downtown Busch Stadium gave Cardinals fans thousands of thrills that stretched over multiple generations. The World Series of 1967, 1968, 1982, 1985, 1987 and 2004. There were Hall of Famers, MVPs, Cy Young winners, base-stealing champions, home-run kings, Gold Glove shortstops, brilliant managers, visiting-team villains and colorful cult heroes. It was there that we saw glorious careers wind through the years and come to an end, and promising careers unfold and take flight. They were all there, from Bob Gibson to Roger Freed to Albert Pujols.

"When new stadium gates swing open, it's an extraordinary awakening. It's time to usher in a new era."

We have a hundred questions: With an open stadium, will the ball fly as if carried on the jet stream to break the pitcher's confidence? Or will the notorious St. Louis humidity drain the life from the batted ball and make the hitters frown? We can only imagine the milestones that the Great Pujols will establish here. Will he reach 500 homers and 3,000 hits? Can he lead Cardinal Nation to the first World Series championship since 1982? And how soon can it happen?

There is only one way to find out.

Meet your friends at the Stan Musial statue.

And walk through the gates, to discover the baseball pleasures of this urban Eden.

10.18.2005

For Houston, Pujols' homer is a wrecking ball

BERNIE BIT • I had my column written. It was something about the despair of another postseason elimination for the Cardinals. And then Albert Pujols wrecked the column, wrecked Brad Lidge, wrecked the Astros. I didn't mind. I downloaded the Spanish broadcast call of this homer, and the announcers went berserk. Makes me smile every time I listen.

"This wouldn't be one of those cheap, dinky homers that have become Houston's offensive specialty at Minute Maid Park. No, Pujols hit a real man's homer."

HOUSTON

With one epic swing, Albert Pujols changed everything. He altered the mood in two cities, breaking hearts in Houston and lifting them in St. Louis.

Pujols terminated Houston's victory party, and kept hope alive in St. Louis.

Pujols took the oxygen out of Minute Maid Park, leaving 43,470 fans speechless and unable to comprehend what they'd just witnessed, a baseball traveling so high and so far that it probably appeared on a tracking system at Houston–based NASA headquarters.

Pujols sent Astros fans over the Ledge by piercing the invincibility of Houston closer Brad Lidge.

With a standup piece of instant mythology in Game 5 of the NLCS, Pujols rocketed a three-run homer that gave the Cardinals a 5-4 victory.

He saved the season, Albert Pujols did.

And, in a move that will please the baseball preservationists, Pujols saved Busch Stadium, at least for one game.

And he salvaged, at least for now, the diminished reputation of the Cardinals lineup in the postseason.

This was some homer.

The biggest of his career?

"Definitely," Pujols said.

Flash bulletin from Albert Pujols to Cardinals fans everywhere: There will be a Game 6, St. Louis. Mark Mulder vs Roy Oswalt.

And there will be a chance for an improbable comeback over the Astros. The Cardinals are still down 3-2 in the series, but that's better than being, say, eliminated.

And all of this is courtesy of The Great Pujols, with some help from his friends David Eckstein and Jimmy Edmonds.

In a ninth–inning rally for the ages, the Cardinals were trailing 4-2 and down to their last strike of the season. Lidge had Eckstein down 1-2 in the count, about to punch out any optimism still left among Cardinals fans.

But the feisty rooster, Eckstein, wasn't about to give up. He singled off Lidge, through the left side of the infield.

Edmonds was next, and Jimmy Ballgame coaxed a walk on five pitches. That gave the Cardinals runners at first and second.

The Astros faithful grew restless.

Up next: Pujols, the Musial of this Cardinals generation.

At the outset of the ninth, Pujols put on his batting gloves — an action of faith considering he was the fifth man in line to bat.

"I just did a little prayer that hopefully I might be the last guy to make the out," Pujols said. "Just give me the strength, Lord, to get one at-bat and hopefully I can come through for my teammates."

Pujols had stranded four runners on base in his first two at-bats of Game 5. And for a moment in the ninth, it looked like Albert was about to raise that ugly count to six left on.

Because, on the first pitch, Lidge made Pujols look foolish, dipping a wicked 88 mph slider just off the dirt. Pujols chased it for strike one.

Lidge came back with another slider, his finest and most notorious pitch.

Pujols was cocked and waiting to unload on a mistake.

Indeed, when Lidge hung the pitch, Pujols hit the ball flush, summoning all of his power and the inner peace of a focused slugger.

This wouldn't be one of those cheap, dinky home runs that have become Houston's offensive specialty at Minute Maid Park.

No, Pujols hit a real man's homer.

"That wasn't no Crawford Box homer, was it?" Cardinals pitcher Matt Morris said. "And who the hell is Crawford, anyway?"

Pujols' blast climbed above those Crawford boxes, and above the train tracks stripped across the top of left field.

The home run was measured at 412 feet, which is either some mathematical error, complete fiction, or a joke. This baby had to carry about 450 feet.

Whatever the distance, this home run surely caused extensive damage in Houston. Pujols postponed or canceled the Astros' on-field pileup, the champagne bath, the civic fiesta, the trip to the World Series.

As the Astros prepared to ice their 4–2 win, Pujols knew it wasn't supposed to end this way, not for the 2005 Cardinals, not for old Busch, not for their fans.

The lights of Busch weren't supposed to be turned off so soon. The wrecking ball wasn't supposed to strike so suddenly. The first blow to demolish Busch wasn't supposed to be triggered in Houston, on an apparent game winning, three-run homer by Lance Berkman in the bottom of the seventh inning.

Berkman's HR traveled only 338 feet, but when it drifted into the Crawford boxes, it must have seemed as if a missile had landed at 250 Stadium Plaza in downtown St. Louis.

The end was not scripted this way, with the Cardinals coughing on their opportunities, until Pujols assaulted that hanging slider from Lidge.

With his team in terrible trouble in Game 5, Pujols stood and delivered. He landed a blow, deep into the heart of Houston, Texas.

Touch history, savor the past, enjoy your stadium memories

BERNIE BIT • I wrote this at the beginning of the season, but now I remember the end. The way Roy Oswalt blew the Cardinals away in Game 6 of the 2005 NLCS to end the season and turn the lights out at Busch for the final time. It was too sudden. I wasn't ready. You weren't ready for it, either.

As the Cardinals worked out yesterday in preparation of their home opener, the sky over Busch Stadium was gray and dreary and dark. And that was fine. It was like having a screen in front of the stage, with blankets covering the props, and the lights turned down low to keep the theater dim until it was time for the drama to begin.

This afternoon, the curtain will go up on the final baseball season at Busch Stadium. And if the area meteorologists are as skilled at performing their jobs as Albert Pujols is at swinging a bat or Scott Rolen is at scooping a ground ball, we're in for a splendid opening day. Forecasts call for blue skies and sunshine, with temperatures reaching the high 60s.

Cardinals general manager Walt Jocketty stood behind the batting cage and surveyed the scene. He pointed to the opening between the stadium decks in right field. "Look at that," he said. "You can see the new ballpark."

Sure enough, the construction cranes are hanging over the new Busch Stadium, reminding us that the days are numbered for the old Busch. As you walk around the concourse today, on the first-base side, you will see the work-in-progress construction of the Cardinals' new home, which will open in April 2006.

And I'm sure that will whip up a range of mixed emotions today, as Cardinal Nation files in, to take a look around, perhaps pausing longer than usual to absorb the visuals, which will disappear in a matter of months. Candidly, a brief walk inside the current Busch Stadium was depressing. The field, the playing surface, looks beautiful. But the interior is deteriorating, and dirty. Sitting in his office, Cardinals manager Tony La Russa talked about some of the unpleasant, plumbing-related odors that are more detectable at Busch. It doesn't appear that Cardinals management invested much money in spring cleaning before this, the 40th and final season at 250 Stadium Plaza. And in a pragmatic way, it

"From 1966 until the mid-1990s — before the grass sod was rolled in, and the bleachers, bullpen and scoreboard areas received a retro-style makeover — Busch was devoid of any real artistry or imagination."

makes sense: Why fix up something that soon will be destroyed?

And Busch has never been romanticized by outsiders, who view it on architectural terms. From 1966 until the mid-1990s — before the grass sod was rolled in, and the bleachers, bullpen and outfield scoreboard areas received a retro-style makeover — Busch was a concrete bowl, devoid of any real artistry or imagination save for Edward Durell Stone's arched cut-ins at the top of the stadium.

In a 1990 interview with the Post–Dispatch, political commentator and baseball observer George Will posed this acerbic question: "How did such a great and serious baseball town build such a hideous stadium?"

Maybe the question should be: Why did so many people embrace such a stadium? Over the past 39 years, nearly 86 million have attended games at Busch. They've watched games in April's numbing chill and been forced to scramble for cover during flash thunderstorms. Most of all, they've endured oppressive, sauna–like heat in the peak of summer. A day game at Busch in August is perhaps only slightly less scorching than sitting in the crater of Vesuvius.

And most of those fans will tell you: It isn't the structure that makes a baseball stadium special. Cardinals fans from St. Louis and around the nation — the team once again has filled credit-card ticket orders from more than 40 states this season — know the baseball experience at Busch is more about people than building design.

Busch Stadium is where glaring Bob Gibson mowed down the Detroit Tigers in the 1968 World Series. It's where Lou Brock made like a thief in the night against pitchers and catchers who were helpless to prevent him from stealing second base. It's where Ozzie Smith dazzled with feats of legerdemain. It's where Mark McGwire dented scoreboards. This is where Pujols started a brilliant career that could make him the Stan Musial of present and of future generations of Cardinals fans. Busch is where Whitey Herzog contoured his team to fit the fast-track turf and the death valley outfield gaps to make a dashing sprint to three National League pennants. And La Russa and Jocketty have maintained the winning ways, with five postseason trips in nine seasons.

"What I'll miss is the number of times we popped champagne here," La Russa said. "And we've done it quite a bit."

Busch was the stage for six World Series played in three decades. This has been the scene of 48 postseason games, including 19 World Series contests. (And one notoriously hot All-Star Game, in 1966.) This is where Hall of Famers Gibson, Brock, Smith, Red Schoendienst, Steve Carlton, Orlando Cepeda and Dennis Eckersley came to work for the Cardinals. These were, and are, the proving grounds for potential Hall of Famers La Russa, McGwire, Pujols, Rolen and Bruce Sutter. This is where another Hall of Famer, broadcaster Jack Buck, supplied the baseball soundtrack for so many summers.

And Busch Stadium is the gathering place for those who love baseball, adore the Cardinals, honor tradition and get a karmic reassurance that the world is centered and balanced just by calling a friend and saying: "I have a ticket for you for tonight's game. Meet me at the Musial statue at 6:30." That Musial statue is our touchstone.

How devoted a baseball town is St. Louis? Consider: On Aug. 21, 1966, the Beatles played a concert at Busch and drew 23,000 fans. Granted, it was raining when the Beatles played, but still . . . John, Paul, George and Ringo were no match for, say, the Milwaukee Brewers on a Monday night in June.

Mark Mulder, David Eckstein and eight other new Cardinals will discover why Busch Stadium will always exist in our minds and hearts. We've had a lot to cheer, and appreciate, over the past 39 years. And this place has brought us together as a community — every last faction.

The interaction with fellow fans and Cardinals players is stronger than stadium concrete. The bond between a grandparent holding a grandchild's hand as they walk together through the Busch gates is more powerful than steel. The memories can hold any stadium together in our imagination, even after it's gone.

Stage fright is hitting Redbirds hard

BERNIE BIT • I honestly felt bad for the Cardinals, that the rest of the nation never got to see the excellent team that entertained St. Louis all summer.

From the St. Louis view, all of the most likely possibilities made sense. Locally the hope and the belief was that the Cardinals would win a competitive World Series, but no one of sound mind would be surprised to see the Red Sox prevail. Win or lose, we were in for a show. This World Series featured two traditional old–school teams representing two celebrated baseball towns. This World Series would be close, and it would be colorful, and it would be good for baseball.

Only one scenario seemed impossible: that the Cardinals would walk onto the big stage and freeze. No, not this year, not in a thousand years of baseball. We never imagined that the Cardinals would play so hard and come so far, only to embarrass themselves. That they'd go down so gently after a summer of fiery pride and purpose, after an early autumn of charging back to win the National League Championship Series, and after winning 112 games by playing baseball the right way, the Cardinal way.

On a dank night at Busch Stadium, under an eerie Edgar Allan Poe moon, the Cardinals became unglued, and their season unraveled, and we did not quite believe what we were seeing. In a humiliating 4–1 victory over the befuddled home nine, the Red Sox all but ripped down the decorative World Series bunting at Busch and replaced it with funeral crepe.

The Red Sox lead the Series 3–0. The Cardinals are down to making promises that they probably can't keep. In an odd twist, the Cardinals will pull inspiration from these very same Red Sox, who beat all odds and rearranged the order of the baseball universe by erasing a 3–0 deficit to shock the Yankees with a miracle comeback in the American League Championship Series.

"We have to fight back," left fielder Reggie Sanders said. "This is a team that has been tough all year at coming from behind. This thing isn't over until the last out. It's hard to believe when you're down 0–3, but it isn't over."

Officially, it won't be over until the Red Sox complete the formality of

"What a downer for Cardinals fans. What a stunning surrender by the Cardinals. And now we know, just a little bit, how Red Sox fans felt from 1919 through 2003."

winning another game, and we see the riot police ring the streets around Fenway Park to prevent Boston from burning down.

Cardinals fans are undoubtedly dazed, wondering what happened to the magical season. Tuesday was supposed to be the first night of the comeback. Instead, it became the beginning of the end.

The highlight was the ceremonial first pitch, with Stan Musial tossing the baseball to Bob Gibson.

If only "The Man" were 25 years old again, just like 1946, when the Cardinals edged Boston in seven games.

If only Gibby were 31 again, just like 1967, when he won three games to lead the Cardinals to a seven-game triumph over the Red Sox.

After Musial and Gibson left our field of dreams, the nightmare began.

On the national stage, the Cardinals turned into Ashlee Simpson.

Cardinals players ran into outs on the basepaths with knucklehead lapses, betraying the fundamental intelligence that made them an admired thinking-fan's team over the past seven months.

In the first inning, Larry Walker tagged up on a shallow fly ball to left field and was thrown out at the plate by Manny Ramirez. But don't heap the abuse on Walker; he decided to bolt when Albert Pujols, who had been stationed on second base, suddenly broke for third, apparently unaware that Ramirez had made the catch. Pujols would have been doubled off, anyway, so Walker took a shot at scoring. It was actually a heads-up play by Walker.

But in the third inning, the Cardinals made a whopper, a Buckner. With Cardinals pitcher Jeff Suppan on third and the Red Sox playing back and conceding a run, Suppan inexplicably stayed put instead of following third-base coach Jose Oquendo's emphatic orders to go. The confusion cost the Cardinals dearly and put this World Series on an irreversible track. Suppan was thrown out by first baseman David Ortiz when he tried to scramble back to third. Instead of allowing a run, the Red Sox had a gift double play. How could that be?

"I shouted, 'Go, go, go!'" Oquendo said. "And Jeff must have thought I said, 'No, no, no.'"

Right then, right there, the energy went out of the Cardinals and their 2004 season.

The big guns of Pujols, Scott Rolen and Jim Edmonds remained silent and unthreatening. Through three games, the MV3s have five hits in 33 at-bats (.151) with one RBI. They're hitless in 11 at-bats with runners in scoring position. Rolen and Edmonds are one for 22, and the hit came on a bunt.

This isn't a slump; it's a plague. And with the Cardinals' more menacing bats reduced to splinters, Red Sox starter Pedro Martinez cruised through the once-feared lineup without resistance, retiring the last 14 he faced in seven shutout innings.

Cardinals fans repeatedly booed the home team.

Boisterous Boston fans showed up for Game 3 in substantial numbers and made their voices heard, chanting to their heroes, raising beer cups as if to salute the imminent end to the so-called Curse of the Bambino, turning Busch into an auxiliary Fenway Park for Red Sox Nation.

A local prominent athlete turned against the city he competes in. Blues hockey forward Keith Tkachuk appeared on Fox during an in-game interview wearing full Red Sox gear and flaunted his devotion to Boston.

The Cardinals are going quietly, disappearing into the mist. They've never led in this Series. You know the karma has changed when Ramirez and Ortiz are making defensive gems.

What a downer for Cardinals fans.

What a stunning surrender by the Cardinals.

And now we know, just a little bit, how Red Sox fans felt from 1919 through 2003.

Cardinals rekindle glorious past

BERNIE BIT • Pressure baseball, at its best. I was basically holding my breath on every pitch. It's why I got into sportswriting.

Twenty-two years and two days ago, the Cardinals won their ninth World Series championship, with a Game 7 victory over the Milwaukee Brewers. Whitey Herzog and his track stars sprinted to two more National League pennants in the 1980s but couldn't capture another World Series.

We didn't worry. The last World Series came to town in 1987, and we were convinced it would return again, and soon. We thought Whitey's guys would run forever. We never thought we would have to wait 17 years for another appearance in the Fall Classic. We never thought that the kids born in the middle 1980s would grow up, go to college, and maybe start families and careers without seeing a World Series in their hometown. We never thought we'd lose Jack Buck before he had the chance to call another World Series and say, "That's a winner," for baseball's most dedicated fans.

Herzog left. Joe Torre got fired. Ozzie Smith and Willie McGee retired. Tragedy and sadness visited the St. Louis National Baseball Club. Gussie Busch died. Jack Buck died. Darryl Kile died. There were happy days, too. Mark McGwire set a home-run record, but soon was gone. Anheuser-Busch sold the franchise. Busch Stadium will be replaced by a new ballpark in 2006.

Through the years, the hunger, the emptiness, intensified. The autumn leaves would turn and fall, and another baseball season would pass, and a proud, dignified fan base patiently would wait until the spring and the renewal of optimism.

On a windy, wild, wonderful night at Busch Stadium, in Game 7 of the National League Championship Series, a new generation of Cardinals picked up the flag. They grabbed that NL pennant from the grasp of the Houston Astros. They ripped it out of Roger Clemens' hands with a powerful double-team pull in the bottom of the sixth inning.

With the Cardinals trailing the great Clemens 2–1, seemingly unable to shake his concentration, Albert Pujols lined a double into left field to tie the score. And on the very next pitch, Scott Rolen scorched a fastball over the left-field wall, for a 4–2 lead. Lightning, then thunder. Clemens was stunned. The Astros were done. And the town was about to have fun.

"Albert Pujols lined a double to tie the score. And on the very next pitch, Scott Rolen scorched a fastball over the left-field wall for a 4-2 lead. Lightning, then thunder. Clemens was stunned. The Astros were done."

Just like that, it was in front of our eyes, so much to absorb and appreciate. The precious World Series of the past, the exhilaration of the present, and the giddy anticipation of a new World Series that commences at timeless Fenway Park in Boston. Cardinals vs Red Sox. Classic franchises will reunite for another grand World Series, inspiring retrospectives of 1946 and 1967. The two best baseball towns in America will put their rich, old–school heritage on display for an envious nation.

When Pujols and Rolen dynamited Game 7, clearing the way for a 5–2 triumph, the waiting was over. The party was on. And 52,140 fans savored the franchise's return to glory. After an extended absence, the Cardinals have taken their rightful position atop the National League. They are managed by Tony La Russa, who no longer will be taunted for coming up short in his quest to guide the Cardinals into a World Series.

"It's an indescribable feeling," La Russa said. "Just a terrific feeling, when you pause to think about the history of this franchise, and what baseball means to the city. We came up short in the NLCS three previous times, and getting beat was hard to take. This has so much meaning."

The Cardinals reached the promised land with their 112th win of the season. They did it after being picked to finish third behind the Cubs and Astros in the NL Central. They did it by scrapping to snatch the final two games of the NLCS after coming home with a 3–2 series deficit after an 0–3 trip to Houston.

And when the game's final out came on a grounder to second baseman Tony Womack, tough-guy Cardinals catcher Mike Matheny bit his lower lip. He didn't want to cry. That would happen later, in the clubhouse, where joyful tears mixed with the spray of champagne.

"When we got the last out, it took my breath away," Matheny said. "We just wanted to win for each other, so much. We wanted to win for our fans. We wanted this so bad that it hurt. I don't know if I've ever experienced such an intense feeling. Just the satisfaction of knowing we got it done. This was a relentless team. This ballclub never gave up. We were behind in the series, and we were behind in this Game 7. But we weren't going to give up. That would go against everything we stood for all season."

Fittingly, in Game 7, the Cardinals gave us a vintage showcase of their baseball style. Long ball. Small ball. Pitching. Defense. Contributions from reserves. It added up beautifully, Rolen said, to "a day you're going to remember for the rest of your life."

Center fielder Jim Edmonds made a marvelous, crucial catch to save two runs. Womack played with the lingering pain of back spasms and grinded out two hits and made a terrific play on a blooped fly ball. Gritty starting pitcher Jeff Suppan squared off against Clemens for the fifth time this season and finally beat him. One day Suppan will be able to tell his grandkids about the night he outperformed a future Hall of Famer in Game 7 to pitch the Cardinals into the World Series — even helping the cause with an RBI bunt for his team's first run. Roger Cedeno came off the bench to deliver the key pinch hit, igniting the sixth-inning rally.

The smooth shortstop, Edgar Renteria, moved runners over twice with sacrifice bunts. The resilient reliever, Julian Tavarez, slowed a ground ball with his broken left hand to help notch the final out in the eighth. He dropped to his knees in pain, and was helped up by teammates. Jason Isringausen, who lost a ninth-inning lead in Game 6, sealed Game 7.

And as he watched the final three outs go down, La Russa thought of so many things. The legendary Cardinals. The doting fans. His players. The team's owners. He thought of his late father, and Kile, and Buck. He thought of his wife and youngest daughter, who were in the stands.

"My biggest feeling was that I didn't want to let people down," La Russa said. "And we didn't let anyone down."

No, the Cardinals raised the NL pennant, the 16th in franchise history. They raised it high, for all of St. Louis to see, and treasure.

10.13.2002

5-year-old steals Cardinals' hearts and lifts their spirits

BERNIE BIT • If you read this column all the way through, you'll come to the point in which Matt Morris is asked by young Kannon Kile where his dad's locker used to be. I was standing there when the kid asked the question. It's the first time I ever got choked up, and cried, in a major-league locker room.

SAN FRANCISCO

After exchanging a round of high-fives and hugs, the young boy broke from the flock of Cardinals. The players were headed off the field after their pulsating 5-4 win over the Giants. But the little guy had his own idea for celebrating a triumphant afternoon.

Kannon Kile did what you'd expect from a 5-year-old who'd spent the day in a big-league baseball uniform: he wanted to get the thing dirty. And so he dashed across the grass and sealed the victory with an enthusiastic slide across home plate . . . safe! Having scored the team's sixth run — too bad it won't count — Kannon trotted off to join the other Cardinals in a joyous clubhouse. Before the slide, he'd been carried out to the field by Cardinals second baseman Fernando Vina. Kannon wanted to know why he was getting the free lift.

"Because you're the MVP," Vina said.

It was a special day for Kannon, and for the compassionate men who wear the Birds on the Bat. The players won a crucial game. And Kannon had an experience, catcher Mike Matheny said, "that he'll remember the rest of his life."

The Cardinals lost a teammate and a dear friend on June 22 when pitcher Darryl Kile died in his sleep in a Chicago hotel room. But Kannon and his brother and sister lost their father. There is no way to ever fully compensate for that void, but the Cardinals are trying. And the truth is, the kid and the grown-up ballplayers probably need each other right now.

"We'd like to think that we're easing Kannon's pain," pitcher Matt Morris said. "But he's easing our pain. He's a wonderful kid. And he's just like DK. He looks just like him. Has the same mannerisms. It's awesome to see him. It makes us happy just to have him around."

Kannon didn't arrive until a few minutes before pregame introductions, and so getting him into a uniform became the Cardinals' latest team effort.

"There were three or four of us just trying to get his belt looped around his pants," pitcher Andy Benes said. "We couldn't get the buckle through there. And Matt Morris was on the ground, trying to get Kannon's cleats on him. We got it done. He looked sharp."

In a way, Kannon has gained 25 fathers, because the Cardinals are crazy about him. It was a natural, to have Kannon take a shift as a bat boy for Game 3 of the NL Championship Series at Pac Bell Park. The Cardinals were down 2–0 in the best–of–seven series. They needed some extra enthusiasm. They needed reasons to smile.

And Kannon Kile was right on time.

The star of the game.

"It was an inspiration having him here," said Miguel Cairo, the Cardinals' utility man. "When you see him, you see DK. And it makes us think of what DK meant to us. We were a close family in here because of DK. And now we're family to Kannon."

Before the game, Kannon was introduced to the crowd of 42,177, and the incredibly classy Giants fans gave him an extended standing ovation. The other Cardinals told Kannon to tip his cap to the fans, and he did it with style, with the sunlight making his blonde hair shine. It was a big–league move.

During the game, Kannon roamed the dugout, encouraging the Cardinals. Several players said he told them, "Don't give up," after the Giants took an early 1–0 lead. And he was there to offer high–fives after home runs by Jim Edmonds, Mike Matheny and Eli Marrero. But 5–year–olds stay on the move, and the antsy Kannon went behind the dugout to hit baseballs off a tee in the indoor batting cage. And when he noticed other Cardinals tossing sunflower seeds to feed a pigeon near the dugout, Kannon chipped in.

"He threw a Snickers bar out there," Morris said. "The pigeon had this big Snickers bar flying at him. I don't think he liked that too much."

It was a tight, tense and turbulent game, and the players said Kannon helped keep them loose with his banter and nonstop happiness. The Cardinals survived the Giants to get back into the series. Kannon gets the win, and maybe even the save.

"It's great that he's with us," Matheny said. "That's exactly what Darryl would want. So this is really an emotional thing for all of us."

After the game, Kannon sat on a table in the clubhouse to hang with the players for a while. And then it was time to go. His mom, Flynn, was waiting, so Morris helped Kannon get dressed. But he will be back in uniform for Game 4.

"I'm keeping your cleats right here, with mine," Morris told the boy. "I'm putting your uniform next to mine. When you come to the ballpark

"Five-year-old Kannon Kile ... had been carried out to the field by Cardinals second baseman Fernando Vina. Kannon wanted to know why he was getting the free lift. 'Because you're the MVP,' Vina said."

tomorrow, I'll help you get dressed. We're teammates."

Kannon looked around.

He had a question:

"Where was my dad's locker?"

Morris explained that when the Cardinals play on the road, the players don't always have the same locker every time.

"But your Dad always had the biggest locker," Morris told Kannon.

"Matt, why did he have the biggest locker?"

"Because," Morris explained, "he was the big shot around here. He was special."

Kannon smiled.

"Yeah," he said. "Special."

Morris picked up Kannon's red bag, and they walked out of the clubhouse, to greet Flynn. And you could hear the players calling out to the boy. Come back for Game 4, they told him.

We still need you.

In his finest hour, La Russa can't hold back the tears

BERNIE BIT • I got a peek of true emotion, raw emotion, the kind that Tony La Russa rarely shows the public. It's my job to be the readers' ears and eyes, so I wanted to share what I witnessed. TLR is a tough guy, and when he sets his heart free, it's stunning.

The Arizona Diamondbacks had been sent home for the winter. And inside the St. Louis clubhouse, the champagne was combustible and cold and ready to be dispensed by the giddy, whooping Cardinals.

Manager Tony La Russa was not ready to join the party. He lingered in his office for a few quiet moments of reflection, away from the spray of beer and the full-throated cheers of a triumphant team. But La Russa's emotions, like the champagne, bubbled up. And he couldn't contain his feelings. Drew Baur, one of the owners, approached La Russa and commented about the remarkable nature of the 2002 Cardinals, who overcame so much personal pain and so many unfair tests to reach the first stage of October's Promised Land.

"This team is real special," La Russa told Baur. "Real, real special."

The instantaneous review of the long journey from April to October found La Russa's soft spot. His hands went to his face, and the hardshell manager got wobbly. Baur moved in to throw a bearhug around La Russa. After the embrace, La Russa turned away, facing the corner. His fingers were still at his eyes, playing defense, still trying to stop the teardrops from rolling down his cheeks. And this would be La Russa's only failure of this wondrous night.

The Cardinals won 6-3 to sweep the NL Division Series. They advanced to the NL Championship Series for the third time in La Russa's seven-year term as manager. And he had the golden touch; his most important moves in Game 3 were perfect.

La Russa made the decision to start Miguel Cairo at third base in place of the injured Scott Rolen. Cairo and the ex-Cub factor worked like a charm again; secret-weapon Cairo had three hits, reached base four times, knocked in two runs, scored two runs and did not err at third base. All in all, it was a pretty damned good impersonation of Rolen.

By playing Cairo at third, La Russa also kept Albert Pujols in left field. The manager fretted that Pujols' concentration would be affected by having to cope with the defensive responsibilities of third base. To La Russa, Pujols seems more comfortable in left field. And TLR's hunch was correct; in the top of the fifth, Pujols erased a potential tying run and ended the inning by harpooning Arizona's Chris Donnels at the plate.

And in the fourth inning, with pitcher Andy Benes batting, La Russa daringly ordered up a suicide squeeze bunt. Benes tried but sent one bunt foul. But on a 3–1 count, La Russa called for the squeeze again. This time Benes putted the ball a few yards in front of the plate, and Cairo dashed home safely with the go–ahead run.

The bulldogs in the Cardinals bullpen weren't going to allow the Diamondbacks to sneak back and prolong this series. The Cardinals went on to post their 100th win of the season. And La Russa's fingerprints were all over this victory, just as they have been all year. And again, the Cardinals came from behind to win. This team's heart remained true.

"This has been an unbelievable year for Tony," Cardinals general manager Walt Jocketty said. "And tonight's game topped it off. Everything fell into place. He hasn't made a bad decision all year, but this was really something."

And Cardinal Nation is noticing. Fans have warmed up to La Russa, who received one of the loudest ovations during pregame introductions. It took a long time for the sea of red to colorize La Russa, but the unusually cruel demands of a punishing 2002 season put La Russa's managing under a special, glowing light.

Jack Buck died, Darryl Kile died, La Russa's own father died. La Russa and trusted pitching coach Dave Duncan kept applying patches to a staff that used 26 pitchers, including 14 starters. The day before the NLDS began, the Cardinals lost their hopeful Game 3 starter, Woody Williams. In Game 2, they lost Rolen. But through each new storm, La Russa kept himself centered and his players moving forward.

"This has got to be one of the greatest managing jobs in baseball history," Baur said.

La Russa didn't want to hear that. His mind was already advancing to the next round. "We have to play as well in the NLCS as we did in this series," he said.

La Russa moved to the door, to inspect the party. He saw the players skipping through the room, squirting the champagne. He saw their smiles and their hugs in this scene of pure happiness. And this is why La Russa has given his life to this game.

"This is the best part for me, just watching them enjoy the reward of all the effort they put into everything," La Russa said.

The players noticed the manager's dry uniform. Pitcher Rick White and catcher Mike DiFelice double–teamed him. DiFelice yanked La

"And then Pujols moved in with a full bottle of bubbly. ... Pujols wrapped his arms around La Russa's shoulders, and squeezed tight."

Russa's hat. White poured a Bud Light on La Russa's head. And then Pujols moved in with a full bottle of bubbly. The chill and the sting made La Russa wince. Pujols wrapped his arms around La Russa's shoulders, and squeezed tight. La Russa wiped something from his eyes. And it wasn't champagne. It was the moment. La Russa was the manager that everyone loved.

A most tragic week
in Cardinal Nation

BERNIE BIT • I hated to have to write this column, for obvious reasons. But I have to say that I was honored to learn later that Tony La Russa cited this column, and used the old quote from Darryl Kile that was included in the piece, when he talked to his team about the need to play on the day after DK died.

"Every pitcher on the team looked up to Darryl Kile as the big brother with the broad shoulders and patient persona. He offered the quiet wisdom of a pitching craftsman."

Shock. Numbness. Anguish. Disbelief. Confusion. Tell us this isn't true, tell us that this is a mistake. Tell us that Darryl Kile will be on the mound at Wrigley Field on Sunday night to stare in at home plate with those steely eyes and grim expression, just before he rocks and throws a swooping curveball that makes hitters curse the very existence of gravity.

Athletes have died in car wrecks and boating accidents and airplane crashes. They have died at the hands of violence. But a prime athlete, age 33, just doesn't go to sleep and fade into permanent darkness, failing to wake up in his Chicago hotel room.

And especially if he's Kile, the toughest and most determined competitor among the Cardinals. Every pitcher on this team looked up to him as the big brother with the broad shoulders and patient persona. He offered the quiet wisdom of a pitching craftsman. He was able to handle their questions and problems and anything that they wanted to bring to him. He was there for his teammates, and that is why the Cardinals were so alarmed when he failed to show up at Wrigley Field on Saturday.

Darryl Kile always answered the call, and when he didn't on Saturday, his teammates feared something was wrong . . . terribly wrong.

Kile died in his sleep, and that is about the only thing about this unspeakable tragedy that makes sense. It is the only way death could have sneaked up on him to take him away in the night, when he was sleeping and unknowing, and unable to fight back with the same type of grit and tenacity that intimidated hitters and inspired teammates.

Kile was a stand–up guy who never backed down, you see, so this was the only way death could conquer him so quickly. The autopsy report will tell us many things, but we are convinced of this much: Kile didn't have a chance to compete. Not this time.

Our hearts just thump and sag thinking about how it ended for DK. If a man is to die at age 33, he should at least be surrounded by the warmth of family and the glow of loved ones, who could hug and kiss and comfort him. And he should have the opportunity to reflect on his life and his deeds, and he should be able to say goodbye to his wife and children, and maybe impart some final advice that could help carry his kids through life. He should be told that he is loved. He shouldn't die away from home, in a sterile hotel room, surrounded by stock furniture and generic paintings. In the final moments, did Kile know? Was he able to think of his wife and their three small children and smile just before the fear took over? It's just too unbearable to contemplate.

The Cardinals have lost a leader. They've lost a friend. They've lost a touchstone in the clubhouse. And on the pragmatic side, they've lost a premier pitcher who could give them innings and victories and everything he had each time he palmed the baseball. They lost his devoted work ethic and his high standards which elevated this pitching staff. Kile was an old–school pitcher who refused to let the big paydays soften his will. But the team's loss is nothing compared with the void felt by his family.

This has been arguably the most tragic week in Cardinals history. The team, and Cardinal Nation, spent most of the week mourning the death of broadcaster Jack Buck. On Friday, Buck was laid to rest, and the healing process was under way. And now, a day later, Darryl Kile went to sleep and didn't rise. A double blow to the heart. A double box of tissues for our eyes. A double order of prayers. Double black armbands on the players' uniforms.

I will say this now: If the 2002 Cardinals can endure and prevail to win the division title, it will be one of the proudest accomplishments in franchise history. And they have the right man to lead them in manager Tony La Russa. He has a firm hand in crisis management. He led the Oakland A's to the World Series championship over San Francisco in 1989, after the Series was interrupted by an earthquake. And last season, La Russa had the Cardinals mentally prepared to resume play after the horrific events of Sept. 11.

Cardinals players undoubtedly are wondering how they'll get through this, how they'll walk on without their leader and friend. They should turn to his personal story for guidance. Kile's father died suddenly in 1993 at age 44. Kile, who had been a mediocre pitcher for Houston to that point, went on to a 15-win, All-Star season that included a no-hitter. In an interview that season, Kile discussed how he coped with his father's death:

"I don't think I'll ever get over it, because my father was my best friend," Kile said. "But in order to be a man, you've got to separate your personal life from your work life. It may sound cold, but I've got work to do. I'll never forget my father, but I'm sure he'd want me to keep on working and try to do the best I can do."

That's what the Cardinals must do now: Take Kile's words to heart. Kile may be gone, but his teammates can still follow his lead.

On Father's Day, Joe Buck wants to make the most of it

BERNIE BIT • I just called Joe Buck out of the blue, not expecting to get hold of him, and not expecting him to open his heart to me. But Joe knew that my own father was ailing (in the final year of his life) and so we felt a connection. We could relate to what each other was going through. I hope that this column, on the day it appeared, helped Cardinals fans prepare for Mr. Buck's passing.

"Joe grew up in the KMOX broadcast booth, sitting nearby as his dad called Cardinals games. Jack would talk and Joe would listen, at least until the day of Joe's 18th birthday ..."

On Father's Day, naturally, I thought about my own dad. He's been in poor health for several years. It's been a rough experience. He lives a thousand miles away, and by not being there for him, I feel as though I am letting him down.

Fathers and sons . . . I started thinking about my friend Joe Buck. I had no intention of bothering Joe Buck on Father's Day. But in thinking about

"In a sense, Jack Buck is a father figure for St. Louis. Generations of St. Louisans have grown up listening to Jack, or following his frequent charitable endeavors. He's family."

my own father, I couldn't help but wonder about Joe and his father, Jack Buck. I admire Joe for many reasons. At age 32, he's the best play-by-play broadcaster on network TV. He's a good guy. Success hasn't gone to his head. But at the top of the list is the way he's handled his father's illness.

I guess all of us who are agonizing over an ailing father or mother feel a special empathy for him. Joe can't go to the gas station or the grocery store or any other place in town without being asked about his father's health. Saturday, while calling the Yankees-Mets game on Fox, his producer Michael Weisman and broadcast partner Tim McCarver surprised Joe with a tribute to Jack Buck during the seventh inning. Joe was touched by the gesture, but he found it difficult to concentrate after that.

I'm sure that there are times when Joe would like to talk about something else, but Joe is never rude, never curt. He politely describes his father's condition, and thanks the inquisitor for his concern. He has been open and honest and gracious.

Joe Buck knows his father's place in this community. And he realizes that Cardinals fans, St. Louisans, are all worried about Jack Buck. They miss hearing him call the Cardinals games on the radio. They miss seeing him out and about.

More than anything, they just don't want to lose Jack Buck, don't want to say goodbye to him yet. We're all pulling very hard for Jack to rally. It sounds corny, but I believe it is true: In a sense, Jack Buck is a father figure for St. Louis. Generations of St. Louisans have grown up listening to Jack, or following his frequent charitable endeavors. And he's family.

And Joe understands that; that's why he's such a gentleman when asked about his dad. But Joe also finds little treasures in these exchanges with strangers; he's been told hundreds of stories about how his father has touched a life or brightened a day.

"For so many years, my father gave all that he could," Joe said. "He'd do anything for anybody. Now that he's going through some tough times, he's getting all of that love back. People are showing him so much love through their cards, their notes, their letters."

Joe grew up in the KMOX broadcast booth, sitting nearby as his dad called Cardinals games. Jack would talk and Joe would listen, at least until the day of Joe's 18th birthday, when Jack left the booth and told his son to broadcast the fifth inning. That's how Joe's career started.

Father and son still spend their nights together now, except that Joe is doing the talking. The mail is stacked high, and each piece comes straight from the heart. And Joe sits at his father's bedside, reading the cards, the letters, the beautiful thoughts expressed by Cardinals fans across the nation.

"It's hard to get through it sometimes," Joe said. "I get choked up, when I read the things that people tell my father. And that's when you realize what he means to so many people. It just makes me even prouder to be his son."

This was a wrenching Father's Day for Joe Buck. Jack is not doing well. He has been in and out of a coma, managing to hold on, much to the surprise of the staff at Barnes–Jewish Hospital.

Jack Buck is one tough man, tougher than any athlete that he's ever described on the air. He was awarded a Purple Heart after taking shrapnel from a mortar shell in World War II. And now Jack, 77, has spent most of the past seven months in the hospital, valiantly battling through a lengthy list of medical crises. He has Parkinson's disease. He had brain surgery, and a tumor removed from his lung. His kidneys shut down. And he's been worn down by infections.

Jack Buck won't give in.

And THAT is a winner.

"The doctors and nurses tell me that they've never seen anyone like him," Joe Buck said. "His body just keeps fighting. His spirit, his will to live, is inspiring. A lot of people would have quit battling a long time ago, and that's understandable. But not my dad."

On Father's Day, Joe wrote a note in a card for his father, and headed over to the hospital to deliver it.

"It's a special Father's Day, but bittersweet," Joe said. "I realize how important he is, not only to me and our family, but to everyone out there who knows him or cares about him. But it's bitter, because I realize that this could be the last Father's Day we have together."

Joe anticipated that he'd stay at his father's side for a considerable time, maybe longer than usual, because each moment is excruciatingly precious now.

"We've had some great late–night talks in that hospital," Joe said. "And my father has taught me something: be thankful for what you have, and don't save anything for later. That's been his message lately. And that's really the way he's lived his life. He did what he wanted to do, and he never wasted a day. And I think we should all take that tack on Father's Day. Be grateful for what you have, and enjoy your father's presence while you can. I love him very much, and I'm thankful that we haven't wasted one second together."

Ankiel gives Secret Service a scare

BERNIE BIT • Just make it end. Stop the fight. This is no fun for anyone to see … that's all I could think about as I was writing this.

Dick Cheney, the Republican nominee for vice president, made a visit to Busch Stadium last night to take in Game 2 of the NL Championship Series.

Secret Service agents assigned to protect Cheney seemed awfully nervous, and we didn't know why. Cheney was upstairs by the press box, away from danger — unless, of course, he made a sudden lunge for the last of the corned beef sandwiches reserved for sportswriters. OK, then it occurred to us that maybe the Secret Service witnessed Rick Ankiel pitching in the first inning. Cheney's guards noticed the heat-seeking baseballs screaming into the screen behind home plate. They saw a 21-year-old rookie pitcher, out of control, losing the grip on the baseball, losing the grip on his enormous potential. Maybe the Secret Service got Cheney out of the box seats and to a safer spot upstairs.

The 52,250 looked on, aghast, as Ankiel took another walk on the wild side, wandering into that same, disorienting, disturbing, off-limits zone where Mark Wohlers and Steve Blass misplaced their promising careers.

Please forgive the poor attempt at humor. We are not trying to make fun of Ankiel's misery in the opening minutes of Game 2, when he appeared to be overwhelmed by national-stage fright for the second time in eight days.

But the Cardinals lost a kidney punch of a ballgame, 6-5, in what was the longest nine-inning NL Championship Series contest in history. It was 3 hours and 59 minutes of agony and ecstasy and all emotions in between.

It was a long game, a long way to an unhappy ending, and the Cardinals faced a long flight through the night to New York. They trail the Mets 2-0 in the best-of-seven series, and now they will walk onto some intimidating turf.

The situation is grim. And the long night is only part of the story. The long night may lead to long-term repercussions for Ankiel. That is why we are trying to smile a little, trying to pretend that this was just a comedic episode in Ankiel's career.

"You don't want to believe that this is anything more than ... just some bad nerves, some bad mechanics. You want to look up next year and see the phenom on the hill, blowing the hitters away."

Because you don't want to dwell on your fears. You don't want to believe that this is anything more than a young pitcher, squirming in the postseason crucible. Just some bad nerves, some bad mechanics, and nothing more serious. You want to look up next year and see the phenom on the hill, blowing the hitters away. You want to erase the damage to his psyche by rewinding Ankiel's career, back to the summer when he had a 1.97 ERA in his last seven starts.

The kid was bummed out late Thursday night. "I feel like I let the team down," Ankiel said.

This is not so. He did what he could. He's a lad 21 years old, and maybe the lights are too bright at this time of the year.

Ankiel lasted 34 pitches. He threw only 14 strikes. Ankiel walked three. He fireballed five pitches to the backstop. He was charged with two wild pitches. He retired only two Mets and gave up two runs before Tony La Russa finally put a merciful end to the absurdity by summoning Britt Reames from the bullpen. Tony was too late.

Reames didn't even start to throw in the bullpen until Ankiel's 30th pitch.

"Rick said he didn't feel the baseball," La Russa said. "But it's the manager's responsibility to put players in the right position. So I blame myself. I don't blame Rick Ankiel. He's too special."

Last week in the NL Division Series opener against the Braves, Ankiel became the first major-league pitcher in 110 years to throw five wild pitches in an inning. Blessed with a 6-0 lead, Ankiel needed a third-inning bail-out, but the Cardinals held on for a 7-5 win.

In his restart, against the Mets, Ankiel tried to calm down, tried to stand firm on the mound without losing his balance again. But his first pitch sailed right at leadoff man Timo Perez's head. And Ankiel could never get his pitches to appear on the radar screen.

Reames came in and pitched from the gut, allowing only one run in 4 1/3 innings to give the Cardinals a chance. And the valiant Cardinals almost pulled it off.

La Russa didn't have a good night. For the second game in a row, he never got pinch-hitter Mark McGwire up to face the Mets in a meaningful situation. We could pick at his bullpen moves, too.

But much of the postgame buzz was about Ankiel's walk into a tornado. You really couldn't see it coming. Ankiel was 11-7 with a rotation-best 3.50 ERA during the regular season. He had some wild streaks during the year, but nothing like these two postseason starts: 3 1/3 innings, nine walks, seven wild pitches, five hits, six earned runs, and only 47 strikes in 101 total pitches.

Did La Russa make a mistake by changing his postseason rotation to give Ankiel the first start against Atlanta? You can make that case. But no one — not Ankiel, not La Russa, not pitching coach Dave Duncan, not a fan or a writer — could have anticipated this meltdown.

Now, the Cardinals will have to put Ankiel back together again. You hope that next year Ankiel will be stabbing the corners with fastballs, making the batter's knees buckle with his looping curve, mowing down lineups with his abundant talent. You hope that the wild child will go away, and that the golden child will return.

Clark breathes fire into Cardinals

BERNIE BIT • What an impact Will Clark made during his brief and bombastic time as a Cardinal. The best thing Clark did? He scared J.D. Drew into becoming a caring, hustling player. J.D. was afraid to disappoint the oldtimer. It was the only time in his career that Drew played hard.

The Cardinals were down two runs to Tom Glavine, down two runs to the Atlanta Braves' history of playoff dominance. Normally if you give Glavine an early lead, he locks the stadium doors on you.

The Cardinals had to jump Glavine before he could seal them off and send this series back to Atlanta tied 1–1. Hope stirred, wearing red, when Will Clark came up in the bottom of the first inning with two teammates on base. Clark, 36, fears nothing. He's too danged old, too danged cantankerous. He has seen too many danged pitches to let anything rattle him at this stage of his career. And that includes Glavine and the divine Braves.

What, was Glavine going to invent a new pitch? Clark has seen it all before. Bring it on, as Clark seems to gesture every time he waves and rolls his bat and stares at the pitcher.

Clark worked the count to 3–2. The deer hunter, waiting for the moment, took aim with his bow and arrow. Glavine tried to spin an off-speed pitch past him.

Nuh–uh. No, sir. Not on this day.

Clark connected and cranked a three–run homer into the Cardinals bullpen in right field. He admired the baseball's flight for a moment, stuck out his chest and made a proud jog around the bases. He would lead the victory parade.

Willpower.

The Cardinals were suddenly ahead 3–2, and Clark's blow was so mighty, so magical, that it kept the rain away. Clark didn't part the clouds, but it was close. His teammates continued the barrage, and Glavine was done after 53 pitches and 2 1/3 innings.

Willpower.

"They jumped out on us early," Clark said. "With the home run, we got the momentum back on our side. We got the fans back in the game, and the guys didn't let up. They just kept the pressure on the whole time.

"Clark fears nothing. He's too danged old, too danged cantankerous. Clark's demeanor, his swagger, projects a stubborn refusal to be intimidated."

Every time we came into the dugout, that was the one thing everybody kept saying, 'Let's add on, add on, add on.' The guys did a whale of a job."

The Cardinals added on, piled on and pushed the Braves around in a stunning 10-4 victory. They savaged the Braves' esteemed pitching staff for 17 runs in the first two games of the National League Division Series. They took batting practice on likely Hall of Fame pitchers Glavine and Greg Maddux, who have a combined 17.05 earned-run average after two starts. The Cardinals, traditionally overmatched by the Braves, have attacked them with aplomb and bombs.

Clark was asked this: After you beat the top two Braves pitchers, what must the Cardinals do to avoid a letdown?

"Go out there and beat their third pitcher," he snapped.

When another reporter offered the observation that Glavine was off form, Clark voiced an immediate protest in his loud, shrill voice: "When are you guys going to give us some credit? Geez. We did it, two days in a row, all right?"

It's almost as if the Cardinals have announced to the Braves, "Hey, we aren't afraid of you."

And the guy who walked into the clubhouse after Game 2 hollering at rookie pitcher Rick Ankiel – "Hey, Ankiel, get me a beer." – has a lot to do with this change in attitude.

Is it a coincidence that the Cardinals freed themselves of the Braves' dominance after Clark joined their side in the trade July 31 with the Baltimore Orioles? With him in the lineup, the Cardinals won the season series 4-3. They lead this series 2-0. Overall they've won their past four games against the Braves.

Clark's demeanor, his swagger, projects a stubborn refusal to be intimidated. Clark and so many of the "new" Cardinals – Jim Edmonds, Carlos Hernandez, Fernando Vina, Darryl Kile, Britt Reames, Mike James – have taken charge in this plot to overthrow the Braves.

This is not serendipity.

It's willpower.

"We call him 'The General' because he's always on top of the situation," catcher Mike Matheny said. "The guy is just a great leader."

To defeat the Braves, the Cardinals needed a dragon slayer. Clark has responded. Clark has played 11 games against the Braves this season, three for the Orioles and eight for the Cardinals. Here are the numbers: 15 hits in 36 at-bats (.416), three doubles, six homers, 12 runs batted in.

"That's why, when he says to get him a beer after the game, you get him a beer," pitcher Matt Morris said. "He usually makes Ankiel get him a beer, but I've gotten him a couple. Will almost reminds me of college, with a senior-freshman type deal. It's all in good fun. He's earned that respect, and that's what you give him.

"He's such a vocal leader in the clubhouse. He has a routine. He makes sure everybody claps his hands before we go out. He makes sure everybody's got their hat on straight. He makes it fun. He just fires you up. He's awesome."

Clark needles his teammates. They tease him back. The exchange isn't for the meek. McGwire recently put a sign in Clark's locker stall: "I am a dork."

Why?

"He's just a dork," McGwire said. "Just look at the way he dresses, the way he talks. That's why I bought him that thing. 'I'm a dork.' That's for Will. He loves it. He says, 'You're right, I am a dork.'

"And I'll play with this dork any day."

One more time, Morris' father is there for him

BERNIE BIT • Though he got mad at me at the end of his career with the Cardinals over some things I'd written, I'll always have a soft spot for Matty Mo, and the kind of guy he was. Just a great Cardinal. In many ways, a kid that never grew up. And I mean that in a good way.

It was Sunday morning, and Busch Stadium was empty and quiet. In a few hours the Cubs would play the Cardinals and the stands would be full. But for now, the place was still except for the two men down on the field, playing catch.

For the first time since his traumatic elbow surgery four months ago, Cardinals pitcher Matt Morris picked up a baseball and tossed it. Softly. Cautiously. Matt flipped the ball to his anxious father, George Morris.

And George muffed the throw.

"I was nervous, wanting to see if Matt had a grimace on his face," George said. "I wanted to see if there was any pain on that first throw. So I took my eye off the ball. Dropped it."

It was father and son, having a catch. Just the way they used to on the baseball diamond beyond the back yard of the Morris home in Montgomery, N.Y., not far from New York City. George would teach Matt the basics.

George would make the 75-minute trip home after completing his shift as an iron worker. He'd bounce into the house and round up Matt and his older sisters, Stacey and Sherry. And they would play some ball.

George coached Matt's Little League teams. The father had dreams, and the son grew up to realize them. George could tell that the boy had a special talent. The baseball made sounds — it sizzled — when Matt zipped it.

"I knew from the get-go that Matt had a great arm," George says. "He always had the best arm on his teams."

Because of the arm, Matt became a high-school star. He became a scholarship pitcher at Seton Hall University. He became the Cardinals' No. 1 choice in the 1995 draft. He took the fast track to the majors.

But that arm, potentially one of the best, came apart at the elbow in spring training. Morris, 25, underwent major repairs. The famous sports surgeon, Dr. Frank Jobe, transferred a new ligament and attached it to Matt's elbow. Morris was done for the season. The Cardinals would be forced to go without their designated No. 1 starter.

In one-plus seasons, Morris had a 19-14 record and a 2.96 ERA. By today's standards, that's gold. But the arm was numb now. It was so cruel. The flow of talent was sealed off, stitched up. Matt's future was in doubt.

George, 55, was in the ballpark in Jupiter, Fla., the day when Matt popped the elbow. But George arrived late, after it happened. Cardinals pitcher Donovan Osborne told George to sit down. The news was bad.

"It was like a knife in my back," George says.

And now, after the April surgery, all Matt could do was wait for the arm to heal and regenerate. It's a lonely time; injured players feel as if they are no longer a part of the team. George would call to cheer Matt up, but the conversation would turn and Matt tried to raise his father's spirits.

"This was a tough blow, because I wanted to really establish myself as a pitcher this season," Matt said. "But once you've got an injury, you have to get it fixed, you have to get better, so you can get back out there. It seems like all the people calling me, and trying to comfort me, were feeling a lot worse than I was."

George was coaching third base one day when young Matt, 12, slid hard into the bag for a triple and dislocated his thumb. George scooped Matt up and took him to the hospital. It was a father's natural instinct, a father's natural love.

"My dad was always there for me," Matt said. "He just taught me a lot of things about working hard, and going after your goals. My mom was the same way. My father always worked real hard. We weren't poor, but we didn't have a lot of money, either. But I would have the best basketball sneakers when I played basketball. No matter the sport, I'd have everything I needed. I look back on it now and really appreciate it. At the time you don't realize what they were doing to be able to give that to us."

When Matt made his first major-league start — April 4, 1997, at Houston — George and Diane Morris were there. Matt was stretching in the outfield and saw them by the railing. He raced over to hug his parents, who fought back the tears. Matt held the Astros to one run in five innings.

The Morris family will be there — you can count on it — when Matt officially returns to the Busch Stadium mound, hopefully next season. George made it a point to be at Busch on Sunday, when Matt grabbed that baseball and made about 50 soft throws, another step on the rehab trail.

"I wanted to be there," George said. "That's my son. I know if anybody can come back from this and be stronger and better, it's Matt. So when he threw the ball again, I was there to catch it for him. It's a feeling that's hard to describe. Very powerful."

When George dropped the ball, Matt smiled.

It used to be the other way around.

"We always played a lot of catch when I was a kid," Matt said. "My dad taught me a lot. Now we were playing catch again, and it was in bigger surroundings, Busch Stadium and all of that. It was the first catch since the surgery, and it meant something to both of us.

"It's like starting over. Now I have a new elbow. It's a new beginning. It's like starting when I was 6 years old, just picking up my glove for the first time and throwing with my dad."

McGwire, Marises make The Big One into a family affair

BERNIE BIT • We were all caught up in the McGwire fairy tale, writers included. This was before we thought about steroids, performance enhancers, unfair competitive advantages, and illicit home-run records. It was the last night of innocence. Rather than bury this event and pretend it didn't happen, I thought it was important to revisit the moment, and see it for what it was at the time of impact. I refuse to pretend that it never happened, just to save face.

With a crack of the bat, Mark McGwire sent a wicked streak of lightning through the night sky. His 62nd home run left the ballpark so fast, so violently, that it was barely a flash. When it crashed down, streaking inside the left-field line, just over the fence, we knew that McGwire had sent a thunderbolt to the baseball gods. He would be joining them now.

Somewhere in the universe you knew that Babe Ruth laughed and bought a round for the house. You could hear Ty Cobb hoot and cackle. Lou Gehrig quietly smiled. And Roger Maris — undoubtedly pleased that such a quality individual claimed his home–run record — politely moved over, and was happy to do it. Mac felt their eyes on him.

"Thanks to Babe, Roger, and everybody who's watching up there," McGwire said later.

The baseball icons on this earth were mighty impressed, too. Some of the most important figures in Cardinals history beamed with pride as McGwire created the newest piece of baseball mythology for this hallowed franchise.

Stan Musial, Ozzie Smith, Lou Brock, Red Schoendienst were on their feet at Busch Stadium, laughing and clapping. McGwire was one of them now, a Cardinal of legendary distinction. Mac's No. 25 could have been retired on the spot. He stands among the greats.

It was a night when McGwire reached up and touched the stars. It was a night illuminated by an epic deed and a thousand flashbulbs. It was a night of big shoulders and bigger drama. History took flight at 8:18 p.m., giving all who saw it the memory of a lifetime.

Mac did it for you, baseball's greatest fans, in the greatest baseball town in America. It would have been a mean curve for No. 62 to fly out of another city's stadium. McGwire adores St. Louis, and St. Louis adores him. It is the most genuine, touching, beautiful fan–player relationship in baseball. The mighty, record blow had to leave our ballpark.

"What a perfect way to end the home stand," McGwire said. "By hitting 62 for the city of St. Louis and all the fans. I truly wanted to do it here, and I did. Thank you, St. Louis."

Mac says he believes in fate, and fate dictated that he slam his way into our hearts, going deeper than ever. And so he came through. Perhaps that's why he hit the first pitch in the fourth inning. Maybe this is why homer No. 62 was his shortest of the season, a mere 341 feet.

Hey, Mac wanted to end your suspense. He wanted to let you celebrate. So why delay? Why wait for a 500-foot bomb to come down? This 341-foot slap shot got the good times rolling. Mac always had an impeccable sense of timing. The time was right, a city was ready, so he ignited the fireworks. Let the party begin.

Oh, what a night. Sept. 8, 1998. Think about it, freeze the feeling, and savor this evening. The wonder of it all will be replayed, and recited, by this and future generations.

We will chuckle when we remember how Mac had to pause on his home-run trot to backtrack and make sure he'd touched first base.

We will recall how the classy Cubs' infield shook Mac's hand as he made his way home.

We will close our eyes and see him stomp on home plate.

We will feel a rush of second–wave emotion when we remember how Mac scooped up his son, Matthew, and hoisted the boy into the air for a ride that was better than anything you'll find in an amusement park. It was time to grab the hankies.

We will see the classy Sammy Sosa trotting in from right field, to congratulate McGwire. Mac's reaction was to wrap his arms around his friendly rival and hug him so hard that you wondered if Sammy could recover to homer again this season.

McGwire blew kisses to the fans, to his parents.

And then McGwire made one of the kindest, sweetest, most generous moves that you'll ever see. Mac spotted the Maris family seated near the Cardinal dugout. He jogged to them, and hopped the railing. He went into the stands to hug the late Maris' children.

Earlier in the day, McGwire had gripped the bat used by Maris to hit the 61st homer on Oct. 1, 1961. The karma in that bat moved him.

"I touched it," McGwire said, choking up. "I put it to my heart."

The Maris family was due for this tender mercy. Finally, the affection and respect that Roger Maris deserved, but never received, in 1961, when he set the record. Maris was scorned, treated as the enemy at home, as he pursued Ruth's 60–homer barrier. His passage into history was joyless.

Thirty-seven years later, McGwire did the right thing: he shared his

"And then McGwire made one of the kindest, most generous moves that you'll ever see. Mac spotted the Maris family seated near the Cardinal dugout. He went into the stands to hug the late Maris' children."

triumphant moment with Maris' sons and daughters. He made sure that they felt the love that so coldly eluded their father. The embrace came 37 years too late, but Mac delivered.

Oh, how he delivered. He hit a record–setting home run, a shot that was so powerful that it went 37 years back in time, to touch Roger Maris. He brought the generations together. He made the bitterness go away. His was a healing touch.

Fear of failure
keeps La Russa on his toes

BERNIE BIT • I'm going to say this one time, and I hope Tony La Russa reads it: We have had our differences and disputes through the years, and at times it's gotten nasty, but I respect TLR more than any competitor I've covered on a daily basis. He's relentless.

"La Russa claims he doesn't have an ego. He points out how he never takes credit for a win and always second-guesses himself after losses. He considers himself an old-fashioned baseball man."

This will not be another panel discussion of Tony La Russa's baseball genius. This will not be about how he came to St. Louis and stretched the short attention spans of wandering players, getting them to play team baseball instead of amassing bulk Fantasy League statistics.

There will be no review of his treacherous journey through the Land of Oz. No words here about the way La Russa restored a winning tradition in this baseball town without pity. We will skip the usual index of his division titles and achievements accumulated in two leagues for three franchises. We'll table the analysis of La Russa's influence in how managers run games from the dugout.

"I have not created or invented one stinking thing," La Russa said.

Fact is, La Russa is bothered by being isolated for this story. The photo that goes with it? This will make La Russa sick. Despite his reputation for being a big-ego guy, La Russa has been allergic to praise.

La Russa got mad at me once this season. It was after I had written something nice about him, declaring that the driving, grinding Cardinals were La Russa's team. A reflection of their manager. I've been covering pro sports since 1979. This was the first time I argued with a man offended by my praise.

"The whole key to your club is your players," La Russa said. "Write about the players. Give the credit to the players. That's the way it's always been. The scouts, the coaches, the manager are all contributors. Our job is to get guys in the right spots, and a good staff can contribute to a healthy attitude. We can help with the atmosphere. The players are the game. I'm just the contributor."

OK, we will not gush over Tony La Russa's qualities, Instead, we will examine his fears, his insecurities. We will explain how La Russa's weaknesses are actually his strengths. And how his daily tenacity may have "contributed" to the Cardinals' first division title since 1987.

What makes Tony La Russa brood?

"Everyone Has A Fear Of Failure"

We backtrack 30 years, to a Class A team in Modesto, Calif., where La Russa is playing shortstop for the Kansas City A's affiliate.

On the morning of a one-game playoff, he barely could get out of bed. Overwhelmed by a sense of dread.

Frightened by the possibility of making an error, striking out, or making a bonehead move.

So La Russa decided: I'll call in sick. Tell the manager I can't play today. The Game of the Year, and La Russa couldn't cope. So he'd tank it. Surrender.

Then La Russa realized something. If he copped out, he would never be able to live with himself. So he got in the car for the drive to the ballpark. By then, La Russa was mad. Ashamed by his gutlessness.

He sped to the stadium. He turned hard into the parking lot. He slammed the car door. Hard. He walked hard into the clubhouse. He ripped off his pants, yanked off his shirt. Hard. Threw his shoes down. Hard. Got into his uniform and sat before his locker, displaying the grim countenance of a death-row inmate. La Russa put on a stone-cold game face.

That's how La Russa overcame his fears that day – by overcompensating. By exaggerating his every movement. By locking into a serious frame of mind, refusing to release himself until after the game. He disappeared into an attitude. He played mental hardball.

Oh, yeah: La Russa hit a grand-slam home run. Modesto rolled.

And when La Russa enters Busch Stadium for Game 1 of the playoff series vs. San Diego, he will be steeled by that pivotal episode in Modesto. His fears will dissolve in hot-blooded passion for his craft. The Cardinals may lose, but La Russa will leave nothing to chance. He will be prepared for every scenario.

La Russa's hard edge is his weapon of choice. He sharpens it daily.

He remembers the sickness in Modesto.

"Everyone has fear of failure at one time or another," La Russa said. "Sometimes you deal with it by calling in sick. Sometimes you deal with it by coming to terms with it. Every time I come in here, there's a scent in the air. An awareness that I try to take into every game. You learn that, having that concern of failure, if you use it in a positive way, it can keep you on your toes."

Did the Cardinals seem more fearless this year? Well, third baseman Gary Gaetti said the 1996 Cardinals are the hardest-playing team he's played for during his 14-year career. That's quite an endorsement.

"Well, I can't remember a flat day," La Russa said. "We compete hard, and we've been hard to beat on days we lost."

Modesto hard.

Overcoming Adversity

The mean streets of Chicago.

When Jerry Reinsdorf hired La Russa to manage the Chicago White Sox in 1979, team broadcaster Harry Caray made a cutting remark: The Sox hired the young, longhaired La Russa because Reinsdorf was too cheap to pay for a real manager. The early years in Chicago were brutal. Caray and sidekick Jimmy Piersall criticized the young manager relentlessly. Fans rode La Russa hard.

In 1982, Elaine La Russa was pregnant with their second child, daughter Devon. "Elaine was so upset because she listened to all this stuff, and because the blood goes from the mother to the baby, I was convinced that Devon was going to be a little devil," La Russa said.

Devon was healthy. And in 1983, La Russa won his first division title. He outlasted the critics. He knew then that he belonged in a dugout. The pressure didn't consume him. La Russa never deviated from his core baseball beliefs. And he took the same attitude to Oakland (1986) and St. Louis.

"I paid all kinds of dues in Chicago," La Russa said. "But all that adversity early, and all that scrutiny in a tough town like Chicago ended up being a big positive to get to surviving."

The battering forced La Russa to grow a reinforced shell. After Chicago, he'd never back down. La Russa's Oakland teams had a style. They made opponents uncomfortable with their power, aggression and attitude.

The brash A's won four division titles, and were easy to dislike. So was their manager. La Russa claims he doesn't have an ego. He points out how he never takes credit for a win and always second-guesses himself after losses. He considers himself as an old-fashioned baseball man, respectful and wary of a humbling game.

Ah, but we know his secret.

La Russa's ego is channeled through the players.

"They're supposed to have one," La Russa said. "They should go out there thinking, 'This guy is not going to get me out,' or 'This guy shouldn't hit me.' You've really got to walk out there like you own the place."

The way La Russa took on Chicago.

Savoring The Challenge

My favorite La Russa scene:

We are sitting in his office late one night. La Russa is at his desk. The Cardinals have just tipped the Cubs over with a dramatic rally, and La Russa is pumped. He is guarded, but now believes his team will win the NL Central title.

"You bring in all of these people, with their diversity of experience and background, and you have an opportunity to come together and compete as a team," he said. "I just try my damnedest to create an atmosphere where guys want to be teammates and where they respect the game and want to play it right. Sometimes you're good enough to finish first. Sometimes you take your best shot, and it it isn't good enough. All I ask is that we take our best shot."

La Russa goes through a fascinating transformation after games. He decompresses. The pregame tension is gone. Winding down after a victory, La Russa becomes cheerful, chatty. He savors the daily challenge of baseball, the constant tinkering to solve the game's mysteries. And when everything breaks just right, resulting in postgame handshakes, La Russa is liberated for a brief spell.

The Cubs have been disposed, and the clubhouse is empty. La Russa is still wearing his full uniform - minus the hat and the shoes. All of the West Coast baseball games are over. But La Russa doesn't want to leave. He wants to savor this temporary feeling, before rising in the morning to raise the shield again.

La Russa flips the satellite-dish control and finds the classic war movie, "Battle of the Bulge." This delights him. He knows the film by heart. He recites lines before the actors speak.

La Russa studies the screen, mouthing the lines, content for the next hour or so. But he knows he will return to the battlefront tomorrow, and the day after, and the season after this one.

Baseball is hell. In a few hours, it will be time, mentally, to go back to Modesto.

At tribute to Ozzie, a spectator has much to remember

BERNIE BIT • Ozzie Smith was perturbed with me at the time, because I'd defended Tony La Russa for playing Royce Clayton at shortstop. But after I wrote this about his Mom, who couldn't have been nicer, the ice thawed. Long live the Wizard of Oz. No athlete got more out of his talent.

"Isn't this every mother's dream? To see a child honored across the nation by thousands of appreciative fans? To see a child attain a level of respect that few professionals can claim?"

LOS ANGELES

The woman in Section 110, Row C at Dodger Stadium was dabbing her eyes. She rocked gently in her seat. Crying a little, smiling a lot. Wiping the tears, accepting hugs from the fans around her. Embracing all the sweetness and warmth of a sentimental night.

You see, Mrs. Marvella Knox mothered the greatest shortstop who ever lived. And only one mom can make that claim. So she's special, too.

Her son, Ozzie Smith, was being honored by the Dodgers as part of his farewell tour. The Dodgers showed highlights of his career, presented a $5,000 check to help his project to build a new baseball park – Ozzie Smith Stadium – at his alma mater, Cal Poly–San Luis Obispo.

The Dodgers played music from the "Wizard of Oz" soundtrack. The video board showed him making a series of dazzling plays, backed by the sounds of "Somewhere Over The Rainbow." The voice of Judy Garland echoed through the stadium.

Ozzie stepped to the microphone, to thank the fans. He was emotional, choked up. But he made the tears disappear – just like so many little ground balls – and thanked the people of his hometown.

"There's only so many ways that I can say thank you for all the joys that have come to me in the city of Los Angeles," Smith said. "I'd like to thank all of you for being a part of my dream to play major-league baseball."

And then he looked up into the stands.

Ozzie's eyes met his mother's. He waved. She smiled. Ozzie slipped into the dugout. Marvella Knox never felt so proud.

"I don't have the words to express this feeling," she said. "I am blessed. You must know how I felt when he was a young kid, struggling to make it. I think of those times, and I see him now, and it's very emotional."

A stranger approached her. It was a woman from Australia, who said she became a baseball fan because of Ozzie Smith. Marvella cleared away another tear. And then came a young man who lives in LA. He shook Marvella's hand.

"I wanted to tell you that behind every great human there's a mother with a heart of gold," the man said.

Marvella's smile could have illuminated Dodger Stadium. Marvella showed a visitor her favorite bracelet. It has 13 miniature Gold Gloves, representing each award won by The No. 1 shortstop.

By the way: Ozzie looks just like his mom.

Isn't this every mother's dream? To see a child rise to prominence, recognized as the best at his trade? To see a child honored across the nation by thousands of appreciative fans? To see a child attain a level of respect that few professionals can claim? To know that your child is loved by so many people?

"Of course, I knew he'd make it," Marvella Knox said. "When a mother knows her child, she knows him better than he knows himself. And he always wanted to be the best. He always wanted to play. He always wanted to be a baseball player. He never stopped chasing the dream."

Ozzie – the second-oldest of Marvella's six children – never stopped chasing ground balls, either.

"When he was a boy, he tore down a man's garage by playing 'wall ball' all day," his mom said. "They were always playing ball. Sometimes, they would take off. And I wouldn't even know where they were. They'd ride the bus and come out here to the stadium and try to get autographs from the players. Nothing would stop him."

And then there was the lumber yard across the street from Ozzie's home.

A significant training ground, as it turns out.

"That's where he learned to do his famous backflip," his mother said. "That lumber yard had a sawdust pit. And he'd tumble around in that sawdust. He'd come home covered in that sawdust from the top of his head, all the way down."

Those were happy days. But not easy days. "We lived in Watts, and it was very hard," Marvella said. "We knew we were in a rough neighborhood, but we didn't let the circumstances get in the way. We did the best we could to have a good family. And we did have a good family, with a lot of love."

Marvella was divorced when Ozzie was in grade school. The children - sons Frederick, Ozzie, Carl, Clodis and Algie, plus daughter Pamela - were all born in a nine-year span.

"After the divorce, Ozzie became the man," Marvella said. "He had the responsibility. He had to take care of the family. He did anything he could to help. He was always taking the leadership role, even though he wasn't the oldest.

". . . You know, Ozzie has always been a great son. Yes, he takes care of me, if I need anything. But this isn't about money. Before he had any money at all, he always wanted you to have a part of everything he had. He's just that type of person. He was precious. All my children are very precious. But Ozzie . . ."

Marvella Knox didn't have to finish the sentence.

She was over the rainbow now, taken there by her own Wizard of Oz.

Raising a toast to a symbolic grandfather

BERNIE BIT • I wish I could have turned back the clock, and been around when Gussie and Whitey got together to drink beer and rebuild the baseball team. Gussie Busch was the last of the old-school owners in St. Louis sports, before everything turned so corporate.

When an important person dies, you go to a saloon in an attempt to understand what his life, and his loss, means to a city. You go there to learn if the deceased was loved or hated, if he will be missed, if his presence mattered at all.

You go to the saloons, or to the bleacher entrance outside the ballpark, places where no public relations men control the reaction, making sure that the appropriate words are spoken in the appropriate tone. Gussie Busch died yesterday and the people spoke from the heart: His life, and his loss, mattered.

In the saloons near Busch Stadium, the people of St. Louis were raising glasses in his honor hours before the Cubs and Cardinals played the 160th baseball game of a long season. It didn't take long for the celebration of Busch's life to commence.

"You know," broadcaster Mike Shannon said, "there weren't too many things that Gussie liked to do better than to duck into a corner bar, a little neighborhood tavern, and drink draft beer with people he didn't even know. He just liked to hear what they were talking about."

Yesterday, they were talking about Gussie Busch. They were raising glasses and toasting his name. They were raising glasses and praising his legacy. The Budweiser flowed.

"Up and down the bar, all day long, people were saluting Gussie," said Trifon Panapoulos, proprietor of the Missouri Bar & Grill on Tucker Boulevard. "This man meant a lot to people in this city. You don't usually hear people talk about someone like they talked about this man today. He did a lot for St. Louis."

Anyone born and raised in St. Louis knows the history. Busch's family kept the brewery open during Prohibition, which lasted from 1920–33. The Busches couldn't make beer, but kept a large workforce employed, and fed, by manufacturing yeast, corn syrup and other products.

Busch purchased, and maybe saved, the Cardinals in 1953. A decade later, he donated $5 million in seed money used for the construction of a

"Jack Buck asked the crowd to stand for a moment of silence. The moment became a minute, finally broken when a man in the box seats hollered, 'We love you, Gussie.' The players from both teams began to clap."

new stadium that triggered the revival of a decayed downtown.

He hired Whitey Herzog.

And Busch showed St. Louis how to have a good time, whether it was drinking beer, leading a World Series celebration, riding horses or racing boats across the water.

It seems that St. Louis has lost something more than a brewer and the owner of a baseball team.

St. Louis, perhaps, has lost someone who was the symbolic grandfather for an entire community.

In the saloons, it was said that Busch personified all that is good about St. Louis. It was said that even if you never met him, you felt that you knew him. After all, he has been in the social mainstream for so long: offering beer and baseball and good times to millions.

"This isn't a glamorous city," Shannon said. "We're not glamorous people. We're good, hard-working people. Gussie was rich, but he worked hard. He had a good time. He was proud, but he never thought he was better than anybody else. He'd drink a beer with you, if you were

"Gussie Busch showed St. Louis how to have a good time, whether it was drinking beer, leading a World Series celebration, riding horses or racing boats across the water."

the mayor or the street cleaner."

Outside Busch Stadium, Pete Elder and Tom Henry, two 50something natives of the South Side, stood in line and waited for the bleacher gate to open. It was three hours before game time, and they wanted to grab two of the best spots. They heard the news about Gussie Busch on the way to the ballpark.

"We loved that old man," Henry said. "Here was one of the wealthiest men in the country and you'd never know it. He always kept his touch with the common man. On opening day or in the World Series, when he'd come through that gate, sitting on the wagon and riding that team of Clydesdales, everyone in the ballpark would go crazy."

Inside Busch Stadium, with 43,570 listening, Jack Buck came onto the field and offered a low-key, tasteful review–tribute to Busch's life. Buck asked the crowd to stand for a moment of silence, but the fans already were on their feet.

The moment became a minute of silence, finally broken when a man in the box seats hollered, "We love you, Gussie." The players from both teams, and the fans, began to clap.

The fans were out of their seats again in the bottom of the seventh, when Busch's image was illuminated on the highlight board. Thousands clapped in rhythm as Ernie Hays played the Budweiser theme song. Here comes the king. Long live the king. And raise the glass.

"I hope," Shannon said, "that everyone will drink one for Gussie."

"We will be talking about it for the rest of our lives ... and it will be passed on through the generations. The tale will be told about a gripping, dramatic, thrilling Super Bowl in Atlanta."

Georgia gave her hometown an NFL title — and a lot more

BERNIE BIT • OK, here's a cliché, but it's so true in this instance: Georgia Frontiere was one of a kind. When she died, I wrote a tribute column for the Post-Dispatch. But I also wrote a blog about her on our website, STLtoday.com. What follows is that combined column and blog on the Rams' first lady.

Georgia Frontiere loved life, and its adventures, more than anyone I knew. She was a remarkable woman. She was eccentric and colorful and unpredictable and never dull.

And what a life. What an improbable and unimaginable life. If you wrote a book about all of her days and nights, people would dismiss it as fiction, except that all of it really happened. This was the NFL version of "My Fair Lady."

No wonder Georgia didn't want to give up, didn't want to leave, didn't want the journey, the escapade, to end. The doctors told Georgia's family months ago that she didn't have much time left, but she battled on with as much courage as the toughest Rams player. She outlived the predictions, outlasted the doctors, and extended that wonderful life until finally succumbing to breast cancer at age 80.

The road home to St. Louis for her final years was a magical mystery tour for Georgia, and her football team. All of the marriages, all the friends, all of the famous pals. Georgia knew the Kennedys. She graciously hosted youngsters John and Caroline Kennedy at a Baltimore Colts game less than a year after their father, JFK, was assassinated. Jackie Kennedy wrote her the sweetest thank-you note. Georgia knew Queen Elizabeth and other members of England's royal family. She hosted parties for Ronald and Nancy Reagan.

She would dine with movie stars and men of letters. She played the piano with Dave Brubeck in the middle of her living room. But before you get the idea that she was pretentious, and A-list conscious, and completely removed from her middle-class upbringing on the west side of St. Louis, I once saw her buy a round of beer and chilled vodka shots for rowdy Rams fans in San Francisco. And she joined them, throwing down the shots with equal fervor. I once saw her lead a rousing sing-along around a piano in a saloon in New Orleans, with her majestic voice filling the place with show tunes, Cole Porter pieces, anything that delighted the crowd.

Georgia Frontiere was also a grandmotherly type who would bake cookies for Marshall Faulk, and send chicken soup to flu-ridden players. She had great charisma and warmth, and was nothing like I expected her to be. After all of the horror stories in Los Angeles, where she had been reduced to the level of a cartoon character, I fully expected a mean-spirited, heartless diva to show up in St. Louis when the Rams moved here. She was nothing like that.

In the time I spent with her, she was kind and generous with people, and attentive to charitable causes. Born as Georgia Irwin, she brought an NFL team back to her hometown, and after everyone in the league dismissed her as a lightweight, she won the Super Bowl. With perfect timing, she put NFL Commissioner Paul Tagliabue in his place on the victory stand, reminding him of his initial attempts to block the team's move to St. Louis.

"It proves that we did the right thing in going to St. Louis," she said on national TV.

Understand this: If Frontiere didn't have the stomach to fight Tagliabue and the boys, there's no team here. There's no Super Bowl championship, or parade. There's no Kurt Warner, Faulk, or "The Greatest Show on Turf." None of it. But Frontiere refused to back down, and her drive to bring the Rams here paid off for her, and for the football fans of this city.

Georgia was sincere in her desire to make St. Louis proud, and she succeeded.

And she also extended the hours of a lot of St. Louis restaurants. When you went to dinner with Georgia, two unknown factors were always in play: How late would she be? And who would be in her entourage? It might be someone like actor Donald O'Connor, who would regale the table with stories on the making of the classic film, "Singing in the Rain." It might be the record executive who discovered Buddy Holly. You never knew. And usually, if dinner was at 9 p.m. you could count on her getting there at 9:45.

Yes, Georgia enjoyed making the grand entrance, but that was part of her charm. It would be appropriate — and I mean this in the most affectionate way — for her memorial service to begin at least one hour late. Georgia was always worth the wait.

Of all the Georgia stories I have, this is my personal favorite, and it goes back to the beginning:

When the NFL finally approved the Rams move in 1995, the team had a Saturday afternoon pep rally at Kiener Plaza, and Georgia appeared at the event. She spoke to the crowd, and then we chatted, so I could gather notes for the next day's column.

It was Easter weekend, so I wished her a happy Easter. She mentioned

"... after everyone in the league dismissed her as a lightweight, she won the Super Bowl. With perfect timing, she put NFL Commissioner Paul Tagliabue in his place on the victory stand."

that she'd like to go to Mass the next day. She remembered St. Roch on Waterman Ave. because she had gone there as a child. She grew up in the neighborhood, near the Delmar loop. As it happens, I live in that neighborhood and have been a member of the St. Roch parish.

So Georgia decided that she'd go to Easter Mass at St. Roch, and since I was also planning to attend, she asked if I'd meet her outside. No problem.

I called the Monsignor to let him know that Georgia Frontiere would attend Easter Mass the next day. He was a bit shocked — remember, the team hadn't even moved here yet — but he welcomed her visit.

I also warned the Monsignor that I'd heard, through sources, that Georgia tends to run a little late.

You probably know what happened next.

The church was packed.

I was on the sidewalk, looking at my watch ...

Five minutes until the start of Mass ... four minutes ... three ... two ... one ...

Still no Georgia.

Monsignor joined me on the sidewalk and wanted to know if she was on the way. I had no idea. He said he'd wait a very brief time, but then had to begin the Mass. I understood.

Absolutely. Start the Mass! You think I want to hold up the Mass? I mean, if Archbishop Burke had been around back then, I would have been excommunicated on the spot.

Another two or three minutes elapsed, and by then I was pacing; so was the Monsignor. I believe he gave me the "look" but I'm not sure. Either way, I thought I was in trouble with, with, someone. I lived two blocks away and wanted to get out of there.

About seven, eight minutes after the scheduled start of the Mass, a limo pulled up at the curb, and Georgia appeared. I suggested that we get inside, but rather than walk to the side of me, or whatever, she grabbed onto my right arm.

This is when I learned for the first time about Georgia's fondness for being fashionably tardy.

And for making that grand entrance.

OK, so we enter the church doors, and St. Roch was filled.

Every eye in the place was on us as Georgia, striking a bit of a pose, made her way down the aisle — with me playing the role of usher, leading her to the spot that Monsignor had reserved for her.

OK, making a big scene isn't my thing. For example, I wouldn't walk Bill DeWitt or Dave Checketts to their seats — but what was I supposed to do, cut and run? My mother didn't raise me like that. I would like to think that I am a gentleman.

I have to tell you, that as much as I liked Georgia, at that moment I wanted to just disappear ... vanish ... dive into a confessional booth ... I'm a tall guy at nearly 6-4, but I wanted to be Mickey Carroll at that point. I could only imagine what the parishoners were thinking, or saying, especially a few of my smart-aleck friends.

No one minded.

The Mass was great. Monsignor invited us to the rectory for lunch.

Leading up to this moment, Georgia had told me stories of her youth in this St. Roch neighborhood. I wanted to believe her stories, but again, I didn't know her. Was she being a phony?

I'd find out soon enough.

She explained that when she was young, she'd often come to St. Roch and visit the rectory. A priest would read Bible stories to the kids in the neighborhood, and give them their instructions as a prelude to confirmation, and she was part of that. Before we sat down to lunch, she explained that in the next room was the study, and then on the other side there was this room, and in the next room you could find this or that ... she proceeded to describe, in detail, all of the rooms of the rectory as she remembered them from many decades before.

Georgia's memory was spot on; the priests' residence was just as she had described it. At that instant I knew there was a genuine essence to her. Sure, she stood to profit enormously from the move to St. Louis, but the idea of coming home also held a powerful sentimental appeal for her.

It was an interesting day.

The postscript: Georgia became good friends with the Monsignor, and when she lived in St. Louis during the football season, she made many visits to the church, and the rectory, along with her companion, Earle Weatherwax. They'd eat dinner at the rectory, and at times would play the piano and sing.

The kids at St. Roch school put on an annual Chistmas show filled with music, and at least for several years that I know of, Georgia attended, and spoke to the children. That church became a part of her life.

So even though I felt foolish standing on the church sidewalk on Easter Sunday 1995, knowing that I was indirectly or directly responsible for holding up the start of Mass, it worked out OK in the end.

When Georgia died, Monsignor Sal Polizzi presided over her funeral service in Los Angeles.

Yes, the same Monsignor who waited outside with me for Georgia to arrive at St. Roch on Easter Sunday, 1995.

Little did I know at the time, but it was the beginning of their strong and lasting friendship.

The Monsignor was there for Georgia at the end of her most fascinating life.

01.11.2004

A conservative Martz?
Why, that's maddening

BERNIE BIT • I remember walking with Mike Martz after his press conference, and explaining to him that fans were going to go nuts over his decision to play for a tie at the end of regulation. This playoff loss was the beginning of the end for Martz as coach.

Twenty minutes after the insane, maddening, double-overtime game that abruptly ended the Rams season, coach Mike Martz was seated on the back of a motorized cart, being driven from the interview area to his team's locker room.

Martz appeared dazed, as you would expect from a man who had just been struck by lightning. The sudden bolt appeared in the form of Carolina wide receiver Steve Smith, who streaked through a flat-footed Rams defense for a 69-yard catch-and-sprint for the winning touchdown on the first play of the second overtime. And by a 29-23 score the Rams had just lost their first game at The Ed since Sept. 29, 2002. The ride was over, in more ways than one. Martz asked to get off the cart. He began to make the long, lonely walk down the corridor.

Defensive end Tyoka Jackson grabbed Martz and pulled him close.

"We're sorry," Jackson told the coach. "You know we love you, right? You know it."

Martz and Jackson parted. Martz kept walking, kept talking, trying to explain why he declined to go for the Panthers' jugular in the final two minutes of the fourth quarter, when the Rams had a chance to score a touchdown that would have kept their hopes and dreams alive.

The Rams were on the verge of a miracle, coming back from a 23-12 deficit in the final six minutes of regulation. A touchdown and 2-point conversion was followed by a successful onside kick. Down by 3, the Rams took over at their 42-yard line with 2 minutes 38 seconds remaining. Marc Bulger completed passes for 20 yards, 13 yards, and 6 yards. Marshall Faulk ran for four yards. Just like that, the Rams were on Carolina's 19 yard line with 37 seconds left. They had one timeout in their pocket.

The Rams were in excellent position. There was ample time to run two or three plays — at least. Surely, Martz would go for the kill. He's Mad Mike. He's the most aggressive play-calling coach in the NFL. When in doubt, he always airs it out. It has never been in Martz's personality to play it safe, go conservative, take the cautious route. He coaches on the edge. Walks on the wild side. The rebel. The maverick. Fearless to a fault. He's the opposite of all of those boring NFL head coaches who play it scared, lacking the courage to expose their necks in defiance of conventional wisdom.

So what was this?

The clock was ticking down, and the Rams were standing around. You kept waiting for the Rams to hurry up and get to the line to spike the ball and stop the clock or run another play. You kept waiting for Mad Mike to come up with a daring call to put the dagger into the Panthers. You kept waiting for Martz to go for the win and give his team a push of momentum into the NFC Championship Game.

Instead, the clock was running out . . .

All the way down to 3 seconds, all the way down from comfort and confidence to surprise and confusion, then to incredulity and anger. You could hear the grumbling, the murmuring, the barking from the stands. What was Martz doing? How did the Rams manage to run only three offensive plays in the final 2 minutes? He ran from peril by letting the clock run all the way down to 3 seconds, and then the Rams used their final timeout to set up Jeff Wilkins for a 33-yard field goal to tie the score. Mad Mike morphed into all of those coaches who have played not to lose.

The Rams did go into overtime, and they did have numerous chances to win, but didn't make a big play. And then there was Steve Smith zooming down the straightaway and racing off to the NFC championship game, leaving the Rams and St. Louis behind to engage in a bitter debate over what should have been.

I told Martz that the fans and media would jump him for his safety-first decision at the end of the fourth quarter. That he would be criticized for not going for the win when he had the Panthers by the throat.

Martz stood his ground.

"After what these players had done, fighting back like that after it looked so bleak for us, I wanted to give them the right to get to overtime and play for the win," he said. "I didn't want to do anything at that point to jeopardize that.

"I knew the field goal was going to be good. Could we have popped it in there for a touchdown? Yeah, maybe so. But suppose we have an interception or lose a fumble? What if there's a sack and we don't get the chance to kick a (shorter) field goal and go to overtime? I just wanted to kick the field goal, take the sure thing and go to overtime. If we turn the ball over there, what would the reaction be? It would be, 'He should have kicked the field goal.' I believe I made the right decision."

It's understandable that Martz sought to avoid a disaster. Bulger had thrown two second-half interceptions and his pass protection was breaking down.

Martz's concerns were logical. I honestly believe that. That said, Martz could have called some low-risk, or even no-risk pass plays. He could dump the ball into Faulk's hands, and let No. 28 make some moves. Maybe go with a quick screen, with a wall of blockers set up, giving Faulk or one of the wideouts a chance to weave through traffic for a score. This is an offense that had tremendous playmakers in Faulk, Torry Holt, Isaac Bruce. But Martz's decision to do nothing and sit on the ball was an overreaction to his worries.

This wasn't why the Rams lost. They sputtered in the red zone all day. Bulger threw three interceptions. Holt dropped a long pass that would have been a touchdown. The offensive line couldn't open up running room for Faulk. The Rams defense didn't show up.

Few will be talking about that today. We will be talking about the day that Mad Mike went conservative. And as he walked into his private locker room, head down, he was Sad Mike now. The loneliest man in St. Louis.

Warner and Faulk are best combo in history of the NFL

BERNIE BIT • I've never covered a better NFL player than Marshall Faulk, and for three seasons (1999-2001), Kurt Warner was as good as any quarterback who played the game. What a pleasure it was to watch Faulk and Warner at the height of their talent.

If Kurt Warner or Marshall Faulk wins the MVP award, it'll be nice, but only a trinket. Greatness doesn't come in the mail, in a box, in the form of hand-delivered hardware. Greatness is what you see on the field, game in and game out. Greatness is what Warner and Faulk do every Sunday.

The Rams punished the Atlanta Falcons 31-13 to run their record to 14-2. And now they'll park this machine for a week of rest, having earned a first-round playoff bye. Faulk and Warner closed strong, putting on another show to bring the curtain down on the 2001 regular season and one of the most spectacular three-year runs in NFL history. Despite getting belted in the throat early in the game, Warner completed 25 of 30 passes for 280 yards and three touchdowns. He did throw three interceptions, but those scratches didn't reduce the value of his latest masterpiece season. Warner walked off the field with a 2001 passing log that includes 4,830 yards and 36 touchdowns.

And Faulk was everywhere. Running the ball, catching the ball, blocking blitzers, spinning into the open field, slamming through the up-front beef for tough yards. Faulk finished with 168 yards rushing, 58 yards receiving and another touchdown. He ended the season with 2,147 yards from scrimmage, becoming the first player in NFL history to accumulate four consecutive 2,000-yard seasons.

"We call Marshall 'Canton' around here," Rams coach Mike Martz said, referring to the location of the Pro Football Hall of Fame. "Because that's where he's going to end up. And he's going to take his place in history as one of the all-time great football players to ever play in this league."

In the 16th game, the MVP momentum may have swung in Faulk's direction. After Faulk dashed off on a 53-yard run in the fourth quarter, the home fans serenaded him with an "MVP" chant, followed by a standing ovation as he departed.

When asked about the seemingly close competition for the MVP award, Rams cornerback Aeneas Williams smiled and said, "You mean besides Marshall Faulk?"

Faulk took a moment to reflect on his personal achievements and decided that they meant little to him.

"It's nothing, without the Super Bowl ring," Faulk said. "The one thing that means the most to me is 1999. Because when you look back at it, all of those (statistical) things are there for others to surpass. The one thing that doesn't ever change is that you won the Super Bowl in that year."

Faulk may win the MVP now, and that's no strike against Warner. I am taking a different track. I prefer to view them as a combination, inseparable. The humble, religious quarterback. The intelligent, resourceful halfback. They formed a partnership in 1999, and the result is a gold rush of nonstop offense, a 37-11 regular-season record and a Super Bowl championship.

Here's what I believe: This is the best quarterback-running back combo in NFL history, at least over a three-year period.

I've tried to recall all of the magnificent pairings. Otto Graham and Marion Motley (Cleveland). Johnny Unitas and Lenny Moore (Baltimore). John Elway and Terrell Davis (Denver). Joe Montana and Roger Craig (San Francisco). Dan Fouts and Chuck Muncie (San Diego). Bart Starr and Paul Hornung (Green Bay). Jim Kelly and Thurman Thomas (Buffalo). Terry Bradshaw and Franco Harris (Pittsburgh). Troy Aikman and Emmitt Smith (Dallas). Roger Staubach and Tony Dorsett (Dallas).

These are legendary players, and classic pairings. But none of the dynamic combos had the kind of peak-form rampages that we've seen over this three-year splurge by Warner and Faulk. And the Rams' average of 523 points during their reign makes it an open-shut case. I ran this theory by my friend Peter King of Sports Illustrated, and King agreed: Warner and Faulk are the No. 1 all-time QB-RB duo.

And to think that the Rams were laboring to win games with the Tony Banks-June Henley tandem in 1998.

"It happens on the field sometimes," tight end Ernie Conwell said. "I'll just stand there and think about how I'm in the huddle with two of the greatest players of all time. Kurt will throw a pass, Marshall will make a run, and the thought will come into your mind. 'Unbelievable. These two guys are unbelievable.'

"The way it used to be here, we'd go into a game thinking, 'We're going to lose today,' or 'Maybe we can win.' With Kurt and Marshall, the feeling never changes. It's 'Hey, we're going to win today.' And that's part of what Kurt and Marshall bring. They're excellent leaders. They're never-say-die guys who always expect to win. And when you have fearless leaders with so much confidence, it has as big an impact as their

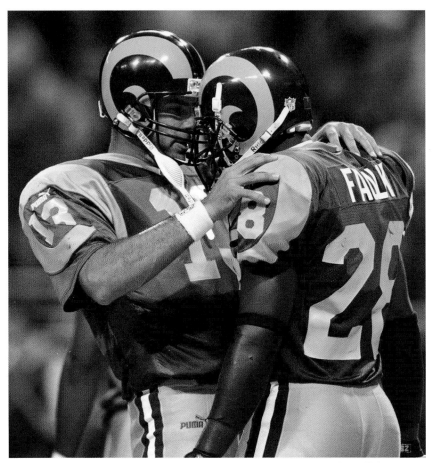

"I prefer to view them as a combination, inseparable. The humble, religious quarterback. The intelligent, resourceful halfback. They formed a partnership in 1999, and the result is a gold rush of nonstop offense."

athletic performance."

Faulk and Warner are too busy carrying the Rams to the summit to put their deeds into historical perspective. But they feel it, too.

"You kind of recognize that you're in the middle of something special," Warner said. "You don't really take that step back and look at it and savor it. But you do understand it. You try to savor just the moment, as it happens. Because you really don't have time right now to step back and think, 'Look at what we've done.' But you do understand that it truly is something special and that you're truly blessed to be a part of it."

And we've been privileged to watch them. These are the glory days of St. Louis football. Appreciate it, while it lasts.

Herzog appreciates gridiron version of Whiteyball

BERNIE BIT • I had this notion that I'd seen these "Greatest Show On Turf" Rams in another form, in a different sport. And I did. It was true. Whitey Herzog filled me in.

Cardinals fans loved the "Whiteyball" Era of the 1980s. Manager Whitey Herzog's teams ran wild and drove opponents mad with their aggressive, high-speed strategy. Whiteyball is alive and thriving in St. Louis.

You just have to watch a football game to see it, with Rams coach Mike Martz playing the role of Herzog.

"I love the way the Rams play football," Herzog said. "And I admire Martz. He's a great offensive mind. He does things on offense like no one else does. He's unique."

The baseball literati used to say the same things about Herzog. Baseball and football are different games, but there's an obvious Herzog-Martz parallel:

They're innovative. Both think outside the box. Herzog cultivated a track-team mentality and won three National League pennants without hitting many home runs. Herzog designed the Cardinals to fit the spacious dimensions of Busch Stadium in the 1980s. Martz's use of motions and formations and his pass-first philosophy go against establishment NFL beliefs. The fast Rams benefit from flying around on the artificial playing surface at the Trans World Dome.

They love speed. Herzog's Cardinals averaged 230 stolen bases a season from 1982-1989. In the three World Series years (1982, '85 and '87) the Cardinals averaged 254 steals and only 82 home runs and were among the top-scoring teams in baseball. Since 1999, Martz's fast, furious Rams have averaged 32.4 points per game. Herzog wanted the speed for defensive purposes; his Cardinals swooped or scooted to the ball to take away hits. When Martz's slow defense collapsed last season, he rebuilt it with an emphasis on speed. The 2001 Rams rank third in the NFL in defense.

Herzog and Martz do not suppress talent; they give their players the freedom to turn it loose. Players love playing for them. Rams Isaac Bruce, Torry Holt and Marshall Faulk know that they're going to get a chance to make plays; Martz won't ice the ball. Cardinals such as Vince Coleman and Ozzie Smith knew they could steal bases; Herzog rarely put up a red light. The result: extreme energy and an aggressive mindset.

Herzog and Martz are perceived as arrogant by some opponents. Martz upset New York by calling for a successful onside kick when leading the Jets 31-7. In one game, Herzog's Cardinals brawled with the San Francisco Giants after Coleman stole second and then third base with his team ahead 10-2.

"When we fought the Giants," Herzog said, "I told (opposing manager) Roger Craig that we don't hit home runs. We run the bases. I told him if his guys agreed not to try and hit home runs, then we'd stop running. As it turned out, it got close and we won that game 10-8. Keep scoring. There is no book. You just use your people and get the most out of them by doing what you do best. You just don't stop in the middle of the game."

Herzog attends most Rams home games and sees the similarities.

"Martz puts pressure on the defense," Herzog said. "He never lets up. And that's what we did. Anytime we hit the ball, we ran like crazy. If we had the chance to take an extra base, we would. If we had the right count, we'd steal a base in any situation. We wanted to put pressure on the defense. If you put pressure on the defense, they get a little jittery. It gets inside their head. And then they start making mistakes. The Rams do that. They get the defense frustrated."

Whiteyball on a football field?

Absolutely.

"I like the comparison," Herzog said. "We believe in the same concepts. I don't know if I'd throw the ball deep all the time, because in football, sometimes when the momentum of the game changes, you need to get it back by slowing things down and working the clock. That's the only little negative thing I'd say about Martz. You can't always go for that quick touchdown."

Well, Whitey never did care for the home run.

'One tackle, and we're on top of the world'

BERNIE BIT • I remember sitting there in the Georgia Dome, watching the fatigued Rams defense fall apart, and thinking that the Rams were letting the Super Bowl victory slip away. I wondered if anyone could step up and make a play. Mike Jones came through.

One tackle made Mike Jones a hero. One tackle made the world spin, made hearts stop, and took everyone's breath away. One tackle turned the Rams into world champions.

One tackle started a flow of champagne in St. Louis and the flow of tears in Tennessee. One tackle forced NFL Commissioner Paul Tagliabue to present the Vince Lombardi championship trophy to Rams owner Georgia Frontiere with millions of people watching. One tackle gave Georgia the sweetest revenge against the league that tried to stop her from moving to St. Louis. One tackle decided the greatest Super Bowl ever played.

It was one tackle, on the last play of the game, made a foot from the St. Louis end zone. It was the final word in the storybook season. It gave us memories that will last a lifetime. It sends Mike Jones, the Rams' outside linebacker, right into that special place where the legends live forever. He's up there now with Bob Gibson striking out all of those Tigers, Mark McGwire hitting No. 62 and 70, Willie McGee climbing the walls and hitting home runs in the 1982 World Series.

We will be talking about it for the rest of our lives, and our kids will tell their kids, and it will be passed on through the generations. The tale will be told about a gripping, dramatic, thrilling Sunday night in Atlanta. The Rams were gasping for oxygen, about to give up their 23-16 lead in the Super Bowl.

We will talk about how Super Bowl MVP Kurt Warner (414 yards passing) recreated a Joe Montana fable with the score tied at 16-16. How Special K released a deep pass just as he was being clobbered by Tennessee end Jevon Kearse. And how wide receiver Isaac Bruce floated under the ball, adjusting in mid-route to pull the pass to his body. And how he sped away, not stopping until he had gone 73 yards for the touchdown and a 23-16 lead with 1 minute 54 seconds remaining.

We will talk about how Tennessee marched down the field. Suddenly the Titans were at the 10-yard line with six seconds left. We will talk

"It was one tackle, on the last play of the game, made a foot from the St. Louis end zone. It was the final word in the storybook season. It gave us memories that will last a lifetime."

about how Titans quarterback Steve McNair threw a pass to wide receiver Kevin Dyson, who caught the ball inside the 5-yard line and tried to curl into the end zone. We will pause here to recount what we were thinking at the moment, in that instant flash of recognition that has yet to become reality. It's almost as if our lives were temporarily suspended.

"Right before that," Rams center Mike Gruttadauria said, "I looked to my left and to my right on the sideline and looked at my teammates. Some were praying, some were chanting, some were holding hands. I think some had their eyes closed. It was tough to watch."

Would Dyson get in? Would someone save Super Sunday for the Rams? Dyson clutched the ball, his long legs trying to shake free for a sprint or a hurdle into the end zone and a likely overtime. It was going to be close. It was going to be one of those plays that separates winners from losers. The history books waited for answers.

Dyson felt a surge of excitement; he was about to score the biggest touchdown of his life. "As soon as I caught the ball, I was thinking 'paydirt,'" Dyson said. "I didn't think anybody would be in the middle of the field."

The Rams were trying to stop Dyson, trying to stop Tennessee's momentum, trying to stop their backs from breaking, trying to hold onto that Super Bowl trophy.

"I was thinking, somebody please tackle him," Rams defensive end Grant Wistrom said. "Please, please someone make that tackle."

Jones was lurking in history's waiting room. He flew across the carpet to make the rescue. Mike Jones, the Kansas City native. The former college running back at Missouri. The former Oakland Raider who was the first defensive free agent signed by Dick Vermeil in 1997. Mike Jones, brought to St. Louis to provide dedication, and leadership. Mike Jones, as first-class a person as you'd ever want to meet.

Jones was about to remind us of the good things that can happen to those who work hard and try to lead a perfect professional life. Jones wrapped up Dyson and wrestled him down.

"There was one tick left on the clock," Bruce said. "And Mike held him with everything he had."

The clock ran out as Dyson lunged, hopelessly, for the goal line.

"That, right there, was the greatest tackle made in Super Bowl history," Rams safety Keith Lyle said. "The rest of our lives, we'll see that shown a million times on TV, and we'll replay it over and over again in our minds."

The game was over. Was it over? Over. Just like that. Are we sure? Yes. Madness. Fireworks. Confetti. Over. They're rolling the stage out onto the field for the trophy presentation. Yes, it was over. Exhale.

"I just fell down," Rams defensive tackle D'Marco Farr said. "I just fell on my back and looked up, just trying to keep that feeling inside. I didn't want to move."

Jones, a quiet man, shook his head when asked to explain his emotions. The sweat was pouring from his face. "Relief," he said. "Tired. It was just like, 'Man, I'm glad this game is over and we're the world champions.' It hasn't really sunk in yet. But I know when I get with my teammates and realize that we're the best in the world, then it's really going to hit me."

Inside the Rams' locker room, Ray Agnew led his teammates in prayer. Vermeil told the players that he loved them. And then the Rams began to kiss the trophy, hug the trophy, take photos of the trophy.

"The entire season, this great Super Bowl, all of the dreams that both teams had, everything we've worked for," Farr said. "It all comes down to one play. One tackle, and we're on top of the world."

Mike Jones lifted them there.

Cursed no more, Rams show they have brave hearts

BERNIE BIT • One of the worst things about sportswriters is how we form an idea about a team, and everyone locks onto it, and repeats it as fact, even if it isn't true. That's how the 1999 Rams came to be portrayed as a "finesse team," in the nation's sports pages – one that would be exposed against physical opponents. Well, it was false. A cliché died as the Rams outslugged Tampa Bay to advance to the Super Bowl.

The story is so improbable, so unlikely, so absurd as to be fiction. The team is coached by Dick Vermeil. He went mad in Philadelphia and had to retire. He needed 14 years to recover. And then, he returned to try it again, except that he lost 23 of his first 32 games. Everyone said he'd lost his marbles again, and he was *thisclose* to getting fired.

The quarterback, Kurt Warner, is a character out of a W.P. Kinsella novel — pure Iowa cornfield mythology. Sat on the bench at Northern Iowa. Got cut by the Packers. Stocked shelves at the Hy-Vee store. Played three seasons of arena-league football. Took a football tour in Europe, hoping that someone in the States would notice. Sat on the bench in St. Louis. Got a chance when the starting quarterback had his knee mangled in the preseason and walked into the huddle with a brush-cut hairstyle and an old-fashioned swagger, looking like the second coming of John Unitas. The running back is Marshall Faulk, put up for adoption by the Indianapolis Colts, who didn't want to pay him because of his moody ways. The star wide receiver, Isaac Bruce, limped through two seasons of hell, with his NFL career hanging by the threads of his hamstrings.

A cast of characters, these Rams are. Chronic losers for a long time. Everything they touched went sour. They were cursed — and cursed at — through nine consecutive losing seasons.

And all of a sudden, it was magic. All of a sudden, Warner is throwing bombs to Bruce, and Faulk is hip-hopping across the carpet, and everyone wearing an official Rams uniform is catching touchdown passes. The defense is sacking quarterbacks and making interceptions. And the head coach is a whole lot smarter.

All of a sudden, the Rams are playing in the NFC Championship Game at the Trans World Dome, with the entire city painted in blue and gold. And it looks bleak, with the Rams losing a dock brawl with the relentless, indefatigable Tampa Bay Buccaneers. The Bucs are winning by the strange score of 6-5, and that old sick feeling — the Rams' plague — is spreading through the Dome. Is this how it would end?

Tampa Bay has the ball. It is late in the game. Warner has turned into a pumpkin. He already has thrown three interceptions. That fastbreak Rams offense has been unplugged and disassembled by conservatism. Offensively, the Rams are playing scared — playing not to lose. Faulk's getting bottled up. The line is getting beaten down. The Rams are running out of time.

"It felt like somebody was writing this," defensive tackle D'Marco Farr said. "It was like: 'OK, if you really want it, you're going to have to scrap for it. All the magic, we're going to take it off of you today. You're going to have to fight for this. We're going to test you. We're going to see if you really want this. Where your heart is.' It was a test."

And then, the young Tampa quarterback gets anxious and misfires a pass. Rams rookie cornerback Dre' Bly intercepts the ball. A few plays later, the Rams have the ball 30 yards from the end zone and the promised land, facing a third-and-4 situation. It's up to Warner now. His day has been dreadful. But this is how you measure the great quarterbacks: You check their heartbeat, their pulse rate, in the pressure of the postseason.

Warner drops back; wide receiver Ricky Proehl has single coverage. The Rams have caught the Bucs in a blitz. Proehl, the team's slowest and oldest wideout, fourth on the depth chart. Proehl, playing for his fifth NFL team. Proehl, who had caught 466 passes in his career. But he couldn't catch a break.

"I've played for 10 years, and the best I've been is 8-8," he said. "Never sniffed the playoffs."

And now, the ball's coming at him down the left sideline, wobbling under the lights. And this is unusual. Counting the regular season and the playoffs, this is Warner's 574th passing attempt of the season. And none of the previous 573 had resulted in a touchdown pass to Proehl. Warner had thrown TD passes to nine receivers this season, but Proehl never got a chance to bob or to weave. But now, it was his turn. A career moment, about to reach his fingertips. If he catches this football, the Rams can trade it in for a trip to the Super Bowl in Atlanta.

"Ricky Proehl catches everything," Rams cornerback Todd Lyght said. "He's money."

This time, Proehl would catch a touchdown with 4 minutes 44 seconds remaining. It was the catch of his life. The Rams were winning 11-6. And after one more heroic defensive stand, it was time to celebrate.

The Rams are going to the Super Bowl. The Rams would have to get there the hard way. They would have to count bruises and welts instead of yards and touchdowns. They would have to wrestle the alligators from Tampa, and the beast chewed them up for most of the day.

The cute offense was put in storage as the two teams engaged in a medieval scrum. This football game was like some of those battlefield

"Warner had thrown TD passes to nine receivers this season, but Proehl never got a chance to bob or weave. But now, it was his turn. A career moment, about to reach his fingertips."

scenes from the film "Braveheart." Rams wide receiver Torry Holt got popped in the ribs and coughed up blood — and returned to play. Wide receiver Az-Zahir Hakim missed four series with dehydration. It became an ordeal to navigate every yard.

The Rams defense never rested. It's one of the roughest, meanest units in the league. Sunday, the defense saved the season. By not surrendering anything more than two field goals — and Tampa had many chances to bust this game open — the defense held the fort until the offense made a late rescue.

This team is more than just speed and a playbook. These guys can hit. They can play tackle football. The Rams beat the Bucs at their game. The Rams may be a pretty team, but they're capable of winning ugly.

"After all the losing and stuff we've been through, it's even more satisfying to win it like this," Lyght said. "Success doesn't come easy. You have to earn it. . . . I've been with this team when we were in the gutter. Looking up at people walking by, spitting on us. But now, we're on top."

The Rams gave themselves and this city one of the greatest moments in St. Louis sports history. And it wasn't easy. It required lots of blood and sweat. And only then could the teardrops fall.

"Standing out there, with all of those guys that you've worked with and bled with and cried with," Farr said. "It was the most emotion I've ever felt. I wish everybody could experience this."

We did.

Vermeil & Shaw: Rams' opposites attract a winning formula

BERNIE BIT • John Shaw had the brilliant mind but probably underestimated the human element of sports. Dick Vermeil probably overestimated the human element. So Vermeil needed Shaw's intellect, and Shaw needed Vermeil's heart. When they came together, a championship was won.

The John Shaw-Dick Vermeil relationship was fascinating from the start. Both have the title of team president, which is peculiar, considering their respective personalities. This is the equivalent of having a liberal Democrat and a conservative Republican share power in the White House.

Vermeil is the light. Shaw is the darkness. Vermeil is the eternal optimist. Shaw is the cynical realist. Vermeil sees the silver lining in the cloud. Shaw sees the cloud in the silver lining. Vermeil relaxes by riding a tractor around his Pennsylvania farm. Shaw relaxes by going to Las Vegas to sit at ringside for major boxing matches. Vermeil drinks Napa Valley cabernet. Shaw drinks Diet coke. Vermeil has been married to the same woman for 42 years. Shaw has been married three times. Somehow, the Shaw-Vermeil football marriage is working. The 11-2 Rams are on the verge of securing homefield advantage for the playoffs. And in the center of the resurgence is the eccentric yin and yang of Shaw and Vermeil. This odd pairing — the lawyer-accountant and the coach-priest — has built a winner.

Vermeil sees players as family. He wants to be the coach and the father confessor, trying to save their careers and their souls no matter how many sins they commit. Shaw views players as commodities to be bartered in the NFL stock market. This is how Shaw came to trade one of his favorite players and people, running back Eric Dickerson, in 1987.

But there's danger in these extremes, and Shaw and Vermeil have balanced each other. Vermeil has succeeded in developing a close, caring, football family. But Shaw has made Vermeil understand that you also need to have talented players to win, and he nudged the coach to get rid of some of the grunts and import some artists. Stars can be part of the family, too.

So the Rams hustle. They work hard. But they also have magnetism and charisma and overwhelm opposing defenses with big plays. Vermeil's warm heart and Shaw's cold eye have produced a potent blend. The Rams are part Vermeil's Rocky Balboa, part Shaw's Muhammad Ali.

Vermeil also realizes Shaw is a master in the art of the deal. Vermeil gets hyper when making major decisions; Shaw is cool and calculating. It was Shaw, not Vermeil, who succeeded in talking the Indianapolis Colts down from their original demands in the Marshall Faulk trade. The Rams got Faulk, the league's best overall running back, for the bargain price of two draft choices (a No. 2 and a No. 5).

Vermeil and Shaw grumble about each other in private, but there is loyalty between them. There was a telling scene in the team's locker room after the Rams clinched the NFC West title with a victory at Carolina.

Shaw approached Vermeil to offer congratulations. DV wrapped his arms around Shaw and began crying. "We did it," Vermeil told Shaw. "Unbelievable," Shaw repeated to DV. The mutual affection was genuine.

Vermeil appreciates Shaw's generosity; the Rams have the league's highest-paid coaching staff and money is never an issue in trying to win. Vermeil consistently praises Shaw, who runs the franchise for owners Georgia Frontiere and Stan Kroenke.

"They've done everything that they said they would do, and even more," Vermeil said.

Shaw resisted the shouts to fire Vermeil after two embarrassing, incredibly chaotic seasons which produced a 9-23 record. Shaw saw enough qualities in Vermeil, the man, to know that he could win. But Shaw knew he had to convince Vermeil to fix serious flaws — or the coach's positive energy and special motivational skills would be wasted. Vermeil's relentless optimism was just what the Rams needed, but Shaw had to get DV to channel it properly. And he has.

"I had full confidence that he'd get this done," Shaw said. "And I never, at any point, wanted to fire Dick. Last season was painful, but it was the right decision to keep Dick. And that obviously has been proven out."

Shaw and Vermeil met Jan. 5 to form a plan to pull the Rams out of quicksand. Vermeil already had fired offensive coordinator Jerry Rhome. He had moved receivers coach Dick Coury into retirement. Vermeil was non-committal about other changes.

Shaw made a case for a substantial infusion. The Rams needed a quarterback. Rather than promote from within, they needed to find a fresh mind to coordinate the offense. They needed a running back. They needed insurance at wide receiver in case Isaac Bruce couldn't recover from a chronic hamstring injury. They needed to find a leader to stabilize the offensive line.

"I just felt we needed to make changes," Shaw said.

Vermeil — who certainly was under some pressure — agreed, because the Rams went on the attack. Mike Martz was brought in to run the offense. Faulk was acquired from Indy. Quarterback Trent Green was signed to a big deal. The Rams won a free-agent auction for guard Adam Timmerman. Wide receiver Torry Holt became the No. 1 draft choice.

Shaw and Vermeil — with crucial assistance from VP of personnel Charley Armey, and salary-cap specialist Jay Zygmunt — reconstructed a team over a four-month period.

I asked Vermeil if his relationship with Shaw had improved. Not that it was bad before. But is it better now?

"Hey, it's better with my wife when we're winning," Vermeil said. "It offsets a lot of problems. And I'm not being funny. It's the truth. People (like Shaw) that have been losing for eight years, and then you continue to lose for two more, it's tough on them. I understood that.

"First off, I knew where their heart was. I knew what they wanted badly to do — win. So if they're mad at Dick Vermeil because they're losing, I understand. I'm mad at Dick Vermeil. My wife was mad at Dick Vermeil. My kids were mad at Dick Vermeil. 'Dad, you don't yell on the sideline like you used to.' My daughter told me that. As if I wasn't coaching. I'm dead serious.

"Hey, we're in a society where people want to win. That's all there is to it. I understand what it takes to win, and I understand what losing does to people, because it does the same thing to me."

Shaw and Vermeil.

The Odd Couple is a hit again.

Going deep: Isaac Bruce and The Miracle on I-70

BERNIE BIT • I've always respected any athlete who speaks of their Christianity and beliefs. But at times, I've wondered if some said it just for effect, to cultivate a certain image. I never wondered about Isaac Bruce. He is a true believer. This was a chilling, amazing story.

His car was out of control after blowing the rear left tire, skidding away from eastbound Interstate 70, headed toward the gully, about to roll over, driver-side first. By now you probably have heard the play-by-play. About how Rams wide receiver Isaac Bruce, who makes a living catching footballs with his hands, took those precious hands off the steering wheel, raised them into the air and shouted "Jesus!" for protection. The Mercedes-Benz flipped twice before crash-landing upright.

Mashed, but standing. Hey, the bump-and-run never could stop Isaac Bruce.

And Bruce, who had escaped death and serious injury, thought of three things.

First, the health of his girlfriend, Glegzette Sharpe, who was seated on the passenger side. She was fine. A little shaken, with a small cut on her forehead.

Next, his own condition. Bruce stretched his arms and flexed his legs. No problem.

And the third thing that came into his mind was pound cake.

Pound cake?

"I didn't even think about dying," Bruce said. "It never hit my mind that, 'I could have died here.' Honestly, I was thinking about getting (Sharpe) out of the car, and how I was going to get my pound cake. I was planning to pick it up that (Tuesday) night."

A star athlete in the prime of his career walks away from an accident that easily could have left him paralyzed, broken, twisted like a pretzel, bleeding, or in a casket. But he doesn't even chip a tooth, get a bump on his head, or rip his trousers.

A Rams employee who saw the wrecked car would recount the scene and exhale, shake his head, and whisper that it's a miracle to have Isaac Bruce still among us. And that maybe this is another sign that the Rams

"Isaac Bruce, who makes a living catching footballs with his hands, took those precious hands off the steering wheel, raised them into the air and shouted 'Jesus!' for protection."

really are a team of destiny in 1999. But in the immediate moments after death took a pass and floated over that Mercedes-Benz and moved on down the highway to visit upon someone else, Isaac Bruce was thinking about ... pound cake?

"It's pound cake that I buy from this lady in St. Louis," Bruce said. "I love pound cake. Every night, I have a slice of pound cake with vanilla ice cream. It's what I eat. My favorite. I was out of pound cake, and I wanted to get that pound cake. And I had the accident, and I knew I couldn't pick up my pound cake."

To all of this we can only say: Praise the Lord and pass the pound cake.

A story worth telling

I know that some readers are turned off by the mention of religion in the newspaper. They don't like quotes from athletes who talk about their faith, Jesus Christ, or scripture. I know this because I have read the letters of complaint on the editorial page, and I have received some caustic e-mails after columns I have written on Kent Bottenfield, J.D. Drew and Kurt Warner.

And that's too bad. I'm going to share this story about Isaac Bruce, and his unshakable belief in God is the foundation. I have no agenda except to tell the story. And Bruce's reliance on a simple command taught to him by his mother — to call out the name of Jesus when in trouble — is how the story begins. And there are some amazing aspects to this wreck on the highway.

There's Isaac's mom, Kairethiatic (call her "Kay"), the mother of 15 children. She has her own testimony about a terrifying accident on an interstate highway. It happened a little more than 27 years ago, when she was six months pregnant with Isaac.

There's the Bishop G.E. Patterson of the Bountiful Blessings Cathedral of Deliverance Church of God and Christ in Memphis, Tenn. It's where Isaac worships during the offseason. Sunday, two days before Bruce's crash, Bishop Patterson asked the congregation to pray for those who needed special help. He mentioned Isaac Bruce. The Bishop did not know why at the time.

There's Isaac Bruce himself: so intense, so gifted, but so mysterious that even his friends struggle to know him and explain him. Something seems to be smoldering inside of him.

And of course, there is pound cake.

"You know, this happened to Isaac before," his mom is telling me over the phone from her home in Fort Lauderdale, Fla. "I was six months pregnant with him. I had all of the children in my station wagon, and I was driving back to Florida from New York. I had a tire blow out, just like he did (Tuesday night). That station wagon went crazy. I couldn't control it. I threw my hands up and shouted, "Jesus!" And He brought that station wagon under control. God spared our lives."

When Mrs. Bruce lost command of her car, it spun completely around — facing the wrong way on the interstate. A truck was headed for the wagon and a horrific collision. But at the last instant the truck screeched to a stop.

"That's why I taught all of my children to call out to Jesus if they were ever in danger," she said. "Isaac learned it before he was even born, and then I always reminded him. So when he had the accident the other night, he was not afraid. Other people might be surprised that he walked away from that accident, but I'm not surprised. Jesus protected him in that car, just as Jesus protected Isaac in my station wagon when I carried him. God gave us another miracle."

Just misunderstood

Isaac takes after his mother. He's quiet, serious and wary of strangers. "People think I'm mean, but I'm just stern," Mrs. Bruce said. "My husband is a quiet man, too. But we're happy people. Isaac is very serious, but he has a happy heart. People just don't understand him."

Isaac Bruce nods.

"People misinterpret me," he said. "They say I don't smile. I smile a lot. They say I always look mean, and that I'm hard to approach. But how would you know unless you approach me? You don't know a book until you open and see what's in there, on the pages. The reason that I'm quiet is, I like to get to know a person first. I like to see what a person is about before I start opening up to them. I withhold. And I watch. The least said is the best said."

Bruce's emotions brewed during the last two seasons, when he missed 15 of 32 games with a chronic hamstring injury. He used the adversity to learn more about himself and others. Now that he's healthy and thriving again, Bruce hasn't forgotten those who doubted his character. But he has forgiven them.

"When I was injured, people would see me walking," Bruce said. "And I'd be walking normal. They'd tell me, 'You don't look hurt to me.' That was difficult to accept. But I'm still the same person now. When I score a touchdown, I still give the football to someone in the stands. Just as a way to thank the fans.

"I know how it goes. Everybody wants to ride the high horse. Nobody wants to ride with the goat. I was the goat for two years. It builds character. I humbled myself. I didn't snap at people, or say anything back. I'd just tell myself that I was still the best at what I did, and it just happens that I wasn't on the field at that time because I couldn't run.

"But I tell you what. I get a little joy walking off the field at the TWA Dome now, and there's a bunch of people who are always there at the railing as we head to the locker room. They're yelling my name. Those are the same people who last year would holler, 'You're not hurt, you stink!' I wouldn't say anything then. I'd get into my car and go home, knowing that they would be the same people, there again, telling me I was great and asking me for my autograph. And that's how it is again."

This is why Bruce hands out few all-access passes to his life. He knows that he can only trust so many people in the world to really care about him and look out for him.

Which brings us to Bishop G.E. Patterson.

Divine Protection Night

Bruce, who attended Memphis State, joined Bishop Patterson's church two years ago. Obviously, Bruce can't be there during the football season. But something unusual happened during last Sunday's service. Patterson felt moved to request a special prayer for Bruce. It seemed rather odd, even to Patterson.

"Jesus will show you the things to come," Patterson said. "I did not have a premonition of Isaac's accident. I want to make that clear. But we were having our 8 a.m. communion service, and asking for prayers. And suddenly I said to the congregation, 'The Lord has placed it in my spirit to ask you to pray for Brother Isaac Bruce. So we ask the Lord to bless him, protect him, be with him.' The people thought it was strange that I would mention Isaac at that time. But the Lord just dropped it into my spirit. God saw what was coming."

There's more. At the same time Bruce and Sharpe were at Hearnes Center in Columbia, watching the Indiana-Missouri college basketball game, Bishop Patterson was in Memphis, participating in a yearly tradition. For the last 20 years, on the first Tuesday night in December, Patterson has offered "Divine Protection Night" at the church.

"We talk about how God shields His people and protects them from danger," Patterson said. "This was the same night that Isaac got in that car to drive home from that basketball game. But we didn't know that. As part of the service, we handed out a gift. Little bottles of blood-red oil, to represent the blood of Jesus."

When I asked Bruce if he had feared dying as the car tumbled over, he wasn't aware of Bishop Patterson's Divine Protection Night, and the vials of blood-red oil — and how it all coincided with the accident. But this is how Bruce responded:

"I knew what the outcome would be once I spoke the name of Jesus," Bruce said. "Once I got that out of my mouth, I wasn't afraid. I knew I was covered by the blood of Jesus."

The day after the accident, Bruce read Psalm 91, his favorite, which says, in part:

"Because he loves me," says the Lord, "I will rescue him; I will protect him, for he acknowledges my name. He will call upon me and I will answer him; I will be with him in trouble, I will deliver him and honor him."

Now we know.

Now we know why Isaac Bruce was so calm as the car flipped over. When your faith is so strong — and so reinforced by your mother, by Bishop G.E. Patterson, by special prayers, by Divine Protection Night, by vials of blood-red oil — you have no reason to fear death. You shout "Jesus" and walk away from a mangled car. And the only thing you worry about is pound cake. Now that's faith. Isaac finally picked up his new pound cake on Friday night.

He says it never tasted better.

Faulk gives Rams the kind of moves they've seen on TV

BERNIE BIT • When the Rams acquired Marshall Faulk from Indianapolis for two draft picks, a No. 2 and a No. 5, it was the best St. Louis sports trade since Brock for Broglio. Faulk did things on a football field that I'd never seen before. And I doubt that I'll ever see one like him again.

ATLANTA

A few years ago, Marshall Faulk starred in a dazzling commercial for a shoe company. He was seen outrunning various modes of transportation, including a jet. Get Faulk into the open, and he's got a chance to beat the speed of sound.

The Rams bought into the image when they gave Faulk a $45 million contract after acquiring him from the Indianapolis Colts for a couple of token draft picks. But for the early part of the season, Faulk was kept in the garage. The Rams waited for the right time to stretch him out. Yesterday at the Georgia Dome, the Faulk in the commercial became a virtual reality. Faulk had his personal Olympics through the overmatched Atlanta defense. He sprinted on dashes. He hurdled bodies. He performed brilliant gymnastic routines. He went on long-distance runs. It was a gold-medal performance.

Faulk rushed for 181 yards and a touchdown on 18 carries. He caught three passes for 32 yards, giving him 213 yards total offense. Faulk had 21 touches, meaning he averaged 10.14 yards when the Rams put the football in his hands.

The Rams won 41-13, and Faulk's multiple-skills clinic left the Falcons so depleted of oxygen that they finally hushed up. All week, the trash-talking Falcons had insisted that the Rams were a fluke. We presume that any unresolved questions were answered by the Rams' second 28-point trashing of Atlanta in less than a month.

"They put up a hell of a game," Falcons defensive end Chuck Smith said. "They did what they wanted to do, and we were at their mercy. They have a strong team."

Befuddled Falcons coordinator Rich Brooks, having to choose the method for his defense's destruction, made the decision to play his safeties deep and take the air out of the Rams' passing game. Brooks dared Faulk to beat them. This was an interesting choice, considering that the Falcons were playing without two injured, run-stuffing starting linebackers.

Faulk saw Atlanta's strategy and put the wings on his feet.

Swoosh!

"Marshall was there. He wanted to run," Rams coach Dick Vermeil said. "He said before the game, 'Boys, I'm ready to take this one over.' And he did."

The Falcons could have chased Faulk all the way to the airport. They still wouldn't have caught him. Of Faulk's 18 rushing attempts, 12 produced at least five yards. The Rams installed a special play for him — "90 flip" — and Faulk hauled it twice for 64 yards.

"It's kind of up to the defense to decide what they want to do," Faulk said. "Do you want to take away the running game, or do you want to take away the passing game? To take away the passing game, they have to rely on their front four to contain me. It's tough. It's a lot of pressure on them to do that. They can stop me at times, but throughout a whole game I'm going to get some runs against them."

When Faulk is in his rhythm, the result is like jazz. You could loop the sounds of John Coltrane, Miles Davis or Charlie Parker onto a video of Faulk running with the football, and his moves would fit the riffs. It is hard to explain his style. You just watch it and appreciate the artist at work.

"Marshall is one of those 'Make you mad' running backs," Rams defensive tackle D'Marco Farr said. "He doesn't hit hard, and he doesn't seem to be running all that fast, but he's always in the open field, making you miss."

Faulk eluded the Falcons on the game's key offensive play. The Rams were leading 7-0 and faced a third down and 26 from their 37-yard line. But Faulk scooted 30 yards on a draw for a first down. The Rams moved in for a 14-0 lead.

It was over except for Atlanta's incessant yapping. Said Faulk: "Chuckie Smith told me, 'Never again will that happen.' I told him, I don't know if it'll happen again but it just happened a couple of minutes ago."

Faulk in open space is one of the most thrilling spectacles in football. He's a threat to score, every time. Few NFL players are as dangerous. This was quite an upgrade, going from June Henley to Marshall Faulk at halfback.

"When we got Marshall here, it was instant credibility to our offense," Rams cornerback Todd Lyght said. "He's legitimately a bona fide superstar in the NFL. No doubt. He's playing like that. Our dividends are being paid already. I was excited when we got him. I played against him before, and he killed us. He killed us. So when I remember watching on ESPN and they said we got Marshall Faulk, I (said), 'Baby!' I was very

"When Faulk is in his rhythm, the result is like jazz. You could loop the sounds of John Coltrane, Miles Davis or Charlie Parker onto a video of Faulk running with the football, and his moves would fit the riffs."

excited."

Faulk did have a 105-yard rushing game against the Falcons in the first meeting, but until Sunday his biggest role had been to distract the defense while Kurt Warner and Isaac Bruce carved them up with precision passing.

"That doesn't frustrate me at all," Faulk said. "I've had the ball a lot of times in the past and haven't won games. And I want to do the things necessary for us to win. Some weeks that means blocking, some weeks that means play action (fakes) to me, some weeks that means being used as a decoy. I know eventually, one of these weeks I'll get a chance to be effective. And I have to hold up my end of the bargain. Today was that day."

The Rams are 5-0. Faulk is on the loose. Yesterday in Atlanta, the commercial came to life.

Streak dies, Rams cry, St. Louis finally has a real football team

BERNIE BIT • Around this time, we were all stirring ... not quite sure that what we were seeing was for real. Could we trust it? Was it a mirage? Would it last? You kept waiting for something to go wrong, to tell you that it was just an illusion. But once the 1999 Rams took off, they never looked back. The skepticism never caught up to them.

After they'd shown the 49ers and the world that they are for real, the Rams returned to their locker room, a 42-20 victory in their scraped, bloodied hands.

The players formed a circle, lowered their heads and prayed. Now it was time to hand out the goodies. Rams middle linebacker London Fletcher is the personification of a Dick Vermeil player. Too small, the scouts said. Nobody wanted him. Nobody checked his heart, either, until DV noticed that all Fletcher does is play like crazy until the last running back falls.

So it was appropriate for Fletcher — who represents everything right about the new Rams — to present a game ball to Vermeil.

"It's about time," Fletcher said, "that we give a game ball to a man who brought these players and coaches together."

Remember, this was the same team that nearly rebelled against Vermeil last season. His practices were long and borderline abusive, and the offense got lost in the sideline confusion and coaching chaos. But Vermeil changed, the offense changed, the karma changed, the player-coach relationship changed, everything changed.

So when Vermeil reached to accept the ball from Fletcher, the players erupted in applause. They love him now. Vermeil, who returned to coaching for precious moments like these, choked up as he addressed his squad.

"I've put some work in here," Vermeil said. "But you players do all the physical work. And our coaches work very hard. This is very, very meaningful to me."

Vermeil in turn awarded game balls to owners Georgia Frontiere and Stan Kroenke.

"You just took my breath away," Frontiere told the Rams. "I'm the happiest person in the world, but I feel like crying."

Georgia cried. Dick cried. A few players wept, too.

"Man, I love these guys," Rams cornerback Todd Lyght said. "This was a long time coming. I just want to thank the Lord for my teammates and this coaching staff. These guys in here never quit. They keep fighting. It was the sweetest victory I've been associated with in my NFL career. I'm so happy with everyone on the team. The way we come together, the way we believe in one another, it's a beautiful thing."

On Sunday at the Trans World Dome the streak died, and the Rams cried. Vermeil got all mushy a second time when 49ers general manager Bill Walsh graciously entered an interview room to congratulate his friend.

"You're going all the way, baby," Walsh told Vermeil.

"Don't say that," Vermeil said.

Walsh turned to the media. "I'm not supposed to smile," he said. "But what a wonderful victory."

Do you want to cry, too? Go ahead. Put the oldie "96 Tears" on the jukebox and do the DV sniffle. All of you. The great fans in the most underrated football town in America. Fans who have been asked to support and watch more bad football than any citizenry in the NFL.

Congratulations, St. Louis. You have a football team. The Rams should have handed out 65,872 game balls — one for every spectator in the house. Your loyalty is being rewarded.

Free the Rams.

The losing streak against the 49ers is over. Seventeen games that can fade into history, never to be repeated again. A sign at the TWA Dome summed it up perfectly: "Ding Dong, the Witch is Dead." And so are the same old Rams.

The 49ers all but hitched a ride on a firetruck for their ride out of town after being burned by Kurt Warner (five touchdown passes), singed by wide receiver Isaac Bruce (four touchdown catches) and blistered by kickoff returner Tony Horne.

The undefeated Rams were so in command that they declined to score an easy touchdown with the ball on San Francisco's 1-yard line in the final minute. They took two snaps and kneeled. They showed mercy, which, if you think about it, may have been even more humiliating to the stunned 49ers.

"I'm so happy," defensive tackle D'Marco Farr said. "I've been waiting my whole career to take a knee with more points than the 49ers had. It was just an awesome feeling. I can't believe it right now."

The Rams are for real.

We saw it. So we can believe it.

Backing the backup: Rams have faith in Warner

BERNIE BIT • I was proud of this column, because I really did believe at the time that this Kurt Warner fellow would be better than expected. I remember having dinner with some Baltimore sportswriters the night before the first regular-season game, and they were making fun of Warner's humble football origins, and asking why the Rams weren't serious about getting a better QB. And I told them – boys, I think Warner is pretty good. Well, Warner threw three TD passes the next day, as the Rams easily defeated the Ravens. Pretty good, indeed.

Fallen Rams quarterback Trent Green had "nightmare flashes" as he tried to sleep late Saturday night. On Sunday afternoon, coach Dick Vermeil broke down and wept as he talked about Green's devastating season-ending knee injury.

"It hurts," DV said. Life with the Rams is painful. Anything that can go wrong usually does. Perhaps the curse started with the drowning death of owner Carroll Rosenbloom in 1979. More contemporary Rams historians suggest that the 1987 trade of Hall of Fame running back Eric Dickerson is to blame for the reversal of fortunes.

My friend Jim Fadler, one of the smartest Rams fans around, suggests that the team's only escape from the doom is to hire Dickerson and make him Vice President of Karma. Only Dickerson can chase the demons out of Rams Park.

For now, all the Rams can do is turn the offense over to Kurt Warner. He was the John Unitas of the Arena League, passing for 10,164 yards and 183 touchdowns in three seasons (1995-97) for the Iowa Barnstormers. Playing for Amsterdam in 1998, Warner was the Joe Montana of NFL Europe, leading the foreign legion in yards passing, completions and TDs.

Unfortunately, the Rams do not have the Grand Rapids Rampage or the Barcelona Dragons on the 1999 schedule.

And it's regrettable that Vermeil didn't give Warner a couple of starts at the end of a meaningless 1998 season, when the Rams had a no-risk chance to inspect his talent and potential. Now they aren't sure what they have in Warner, who has played in one regular-season NFL game.

Still, Warner may surprise us. He's 28 and has played a lot of football. He's mastered many playbooks. And at every stop, he's made plays. He's handled personal and professional adversity with admirable poise. He's served an apprenticeship. His teammates respect him.

And given the fluctuating performance levels of NFL quarterbacks, who can possibly predict what's to come with Warner? At this time last year, did anyone believe Trent Green would be an NFL star, making more than $4 million a year? Green was summoned out of obscurity, and exceeded expectations.

"There are definitely some parallels," Green said. "We each had a different road to get to where we are now. It's going to be a big challenge for Kurt. I think he's ready for it, and I think he can handle it. He's prepared well, mentally and physically. It's just a matter of having the support of his teammates and the support of the fans. Give him a chance. When I finally got my start, that's all I was looking for. Just give me a chance. Fortunately I was able to produce, and I think Kurt will also."

You can't judge QBs on their backgrounds. Unitas was playing semipro football with the Bloomfield (Pa.) Rams when the Colts signed him in 1956. Montana was a third-round draft choice. Dave Krieg, who started for more than a dozen NFL seasons, played at Milton College, which no longer exists. Jim Hart, the best quarterback in St. Louis NFL history, was an undrafted free agent out of Southern Illinois-Carbondale.

Obviously, the Rams were going to put the best spin on the situation, but by late Sunday their dark mood had lifted. Part of that comes from their quiet faith in Warner.

"Warner has never gotten an opportunity," Vermeil said. "He's earned this. We will play good football with him at quarterback."

Remember, Warner doesn't need to be a hero. He's surrounded by wonderful talent; all he needs to do is a competent job of getting the ball to Isaac Bruce, Marshall Faulk and Torry Holt. And they'll do the rest. Everyone loves an underdog, and Warner qualifies. It's time to rally around the Barnstormer.

A new era:
You can go home again

BERNIE BIT • St. Louis is an underrated football town, and I got tired (angry, even) of hearing that an NFL team would never thrive here. St. Louis football fans just needed hope, a reason to believe. And they would respond. This was for all of the fans that were forgotten on those fall NFL Sundays.

"Welcome home to the new fans, who were in high school or college when pro football moved away in 1988. Welcome home to the smallest and most impressionable fans, the kids, who will grow up with this team ..."

As you make that long walk from the parking lot to attend the celebration at Busch Stadium, appreciate each and every step you take on the way to your seat for the noon kickoff.

This is the last mile in a marathon, the last leg in an incredible journey back to the National Football League. These are the final steps home. We staggered, went off course, broke down, blistered, veered down the wrong path, hallucinated, and spent too much money to count. We stopped along the way to build a $260 million stadium, launch a massive PR campaign, kiss Paul Tagliabue and the NFL owners, hiss Paul Tagliabue and the NFL owners, and fight a vicious, hurtful civic war that killed the expansion St. Louis Stallions.

And this long, winding and expensive stretch of road has finally delivered us to the Rams' first home game, an event that opens a new era for football, and sports, in St. Louis. So think about each step you take as you approach the stadium.

The Rams will play the New Orleans Saints, but this is no ordinary football game. This is history. This is a seminal event. This ranks up there with the Cardinals in the World Series, the opening of Busch Stadium, the debut of the Blues, the unveiling of Kiel Center and every other landmark occasion in St. Louis sports. The atmosphere will be charged by currents of powerful emotions.

"I can't wait to get down there to the stadium and play this game," Rams defensive tackle D'Marco Farr said. "I can't wait. It's going to be unbelievable."

Welcome, all of you.

Welcome home to the faithful football Cardinals fans, who never were rewarded for their patience and loyalty. You never lost hope. You never let the flame die. You deserve this.

Welcome home to the fine men who played so hard for those Cardinals teams, laboring to make something good happen, only to limp away from their game, their noble efforts largely wasted by a futile franchise. You will not fade away, gentlemen. A new team will help revive old memories. You will be remembered.

Welcome home to the new fans, who were in high school or college when pro football moved away in 1988. You've never had a team. You don't know what it's like to wake up on a Monday morning and hop out of bed, ready to take on the world, invigorated because your team won. You don't know what it's like to wake up on a Monday morning and move slowly through the day, mind and spirit dragging, because your team lost on Sunday. These are the real emotions of sport. Congratulations.

Welcome home to the smallest and most impressionable fans, the kids, who will grow up with this team, drawing so many childhood memories from these Sunday afternoons. So remove those Dallas Cowboys photos from the wall in the bedroom, little ones, and hang a Jerome Bettis poster over the bed. This franchise is for you. You — not the adults — will form the sentimental bond and create the tradition that truly turns the Los Angeles Rams into the St. Louis Rams.

Welcome home to those who bought the personal seat licenses, making a sacrifice to fund the most expensive transaction in the history of St. Louis sports. And this wasn't supposed to be a football town, right?

Welcome home to all of you who gathered before your TV sets and saw one NFL expansion team go to Carolina, then another to Jacksonville, and resisted the urge to throw a brick through Tagliabue's image on the television screen.

(The worst moment for me was seeing Tagliabue hold up that hideous, mouthwash-colored Jaguars jersey in a Chicago ballroom as he welcomed backwater Jacksonville to the NFL. The second-worst moment was when the NFL owners — in a cheap attempt to extort cash from the Rams and St. Louis — voted "no" on the proposed move.)

Welcome home to Jerry Clinton, who carried the torch that created the lights at the new Trans World Dome. Welcome home to Dick Gephardt, Buzz Westfall and Freeman Bosley Jr., the politicians who quietly convened in the darkest days (post-expansion) to map out a successful strategy to recruit the Rams. Welcome home to Chuck Knight and Civic Progress, who got behind the pitch to the Rams.

Welcome home to The Senator, Tom Eagleton, who closed the deal like a true liberal: by spending a lot of money, and doing so with grace and humor. Welcome home to Rams president John Shaw, so skilled a negotiator that he could sell Coors beer to August Busch III. Welcome home to Rams vice chairman Stan Kroenke, who put up much of his own fortune to make this move possible.

Welcome home to coach Rich Brooks and the Rams players, who are finally getting to know why so many athletes come here and never leave.

"It feels like home," Farr said. "We've got a pretty good settlement now. We rounded up the wagons. We've pitched a tent. We're here. It's nice to meet everybody, and to see them excited about the team. The cable guy came out to fix the cable, and he wanted to know if we were ready to play. The people of St. Louis have gone out of their way to make us feel wanted."

Finally, a welcome home to Georgia Irwin, who spent her youth in a house not far off the Delmar Loop, going to movies at the Pageant Theater, having a cone at the Greenlea Ice Cream Parlor and skating at Winter Garden.

She is Georgia Frontiere now. The fans of St. Louis have made her wealthy, treated her warmly. Today, Georgia begins to fulfill her promise to those fans: repaying their support by making a total commitment to winning football.

This is the day we've waited for.

So savor each step to the stadium gates.

You're almost there.

Welcome to The Homecoming.

"The Blues had the misfortune of playing their usual brand of reliable hockey during a unique period in the city's sports history. The Blues were overlooked, skating in the right place at the wrong time. For all of their sturdy consistency, the Blues couldn't compete with high drama supplied by the Cardinals and Rams."

Slap Al MacInnis on the back and thank him

BERNIE BIT • I respect Al MacInnis more than any pro athlete I've covered in St. Louis. He represents the old-fashioned ideals of professionalism, class, dedication to excellence. And what a shot.

The testimonials arrived from all parts of North America, from the former coaches and teammates, from old friends and fans, from the hard-nosed hockey columnists in Canada, and from the woman who shares his life.

Goaltenders were silent, however. They were undoubtedly in a private place, offering a quiet thanks to the hockey gods, relieved that they'll no longer be required to expose their bodies to his 100 mph slap shot.

As Al MacInnis unplugs that booming shot and leaves the rink, he departs as one of the greatest and most respected defensemen in NHL history. And that is only half of it. MacInnis the man is even more cherished than the hockey player. It was an honor to have him in a Blues sweater for 10 seasons.

Successful athletes make millions of dollars and take a considerable financial portfolio into retirement. But when a prominent athlete retires, the most important thing he takes with him is his name and reputation. The currency of respect. And that defines how he'll be remembered.

You could search through the 50 United States and the 10 Canadian provinces and not find a single non-goaltender to mutter a bad word about Al MacInnis. For those who never followed hockey and really don't know MacInnis, please allow me to try to frame it this way: If there's a hockey version of Stan Musial, it's Al MacInnis. Minus the harmonica.

"You can count on Al," his wife, Jackie, said. "He cares about doing things the right way. He cares about what people think. He has such high standards for everything he does. He's always there for the people who need him."

Al MacInnis had a big shot but was never a Big Shot.

"A great person, a great family man, a great competitor, a great leader," former teammate Doug Weight said. "Hard working and humble, completely unselfish, generous with anyone who needed him. There's a lot of terrific people in the sports world with a lot of qualities, but Al MacInnis rated a 10 in everything, and that's amazing."

With tears in her eyes, Jackie MacInnis watched her husband's official retirement ceremony at Savvis Center. MacInnis, 42, had no choice. A damaged left eye obstructs his peripheral vision, leaving him vulnerable to hits from the side. He'd risk being in the awkward position of fumbling around for a puck he couldn't clearly see.

It was time. Still, it's never easy. MacInnis wasn't able to end his career on his terms. The eye injury cost him most of a season, and that was followed by the NHL lockout and an entire season lost.

So on Friday, Al cried, Jackie cried. Their oldest son, Carson, spoke for all of St. Louis when he said, "It was kind of sad. It's not been a lot of times that I've have seen him sad."

Well, there is some good news. Jackie and the four children (ages 4 to 13) won't be losing him again to the hard road of the hockey life. MacInnis can continue to coach two of his sons' hockey teams. He will work for the Blues, starting out by learning all aspects of the hockey operation.

The Blues are experiencing hard times. The team is for sale. The future of the franchise is unsettled. The lockout hurt the sport's popularity. Chris Pronger was traded to Edmonton, and now MacInnis is gone.

There is no question that one day, when the kids are older, Al MacInnis will want to coach. And by all accounts, he will make an excellent coach. He's intelligent, he commands respect, he can teach, he can communicate.

Players revere him. As a Blues captain, MacInnis was tough behind closed doors but never embarrassed a teammate publicly, and that style generated unanimous loyalty inside the locker room.

The Blues will need that again.

They will need Al MacInnis.

"Flawless career, flawless person," Blues president Mark Sauer said.

"For those who never followed hockey and really don't know MacInnis, please allow me to frame it this way: If there's a hockey version of Stan Musial, it's Al MacInnis. Minus the harmonica."

"Players revere him. As a Blues captain, MacInnis was tough behind closed doors but never embarrassed a teammate publicly, and that style generated unanimous loyalty inside the locker room."

The call finally comes for Federko

BERNIE BIT • Even now, though he's prominent in his role as a TV analyst, Bernie Federko remains underappreciated as a true St. Louis sports icon. I don't think we appreciate all that he did to keep hockey going in this town. Just a good guy, one of my personal favorites.

"As he kept getting shut out, Federko's emotional wounds deepened, but he resisted the urge to lash out. He reacted to each snub with admirable diplomacy."

As he enters the hockey Hall of Fame, Bernie Federko becomes the No. 1 star of the Blues franchise. A great guy with a true-Blue heart is finally getting his reward. And this full appreciation is long overdue.

Federko, while certainly appreciated in St. Louis, has also been overlooked. During his outstanding career, he never was quite as popular as teammate Brian Sutter. That's understandable, because Sutter personified the relentless work ethic that made hockey so appealing to the Saturday-night crowds that filled The Arena. Federko was more subtle and creative. And though Federko's soft, deft hands produced a franchise-record 1,073 career points, they didn't generate as much noise as Sutter's hard-hitting shoulders.

And then Brett Hull came to town to glamorize the Blues. There's been a lot of talk about how Hull saved hockey in St. Louis. About how Hull transformed the franchise. About how he built the Savvis Center. There's some truth in all of that; the intent here is not to disparage Hull. But Brett wouldn't have made his valuable, franchise-altering impact to the Blues without Federko building a bridge that connected different eras.

Bernie's play, his star power, and his strong presence in the community, kept the Blues viable through some hard times. Through much of Federko's career, the Blues operated on the cheap. There was chaos on the ownership level; the franchise nearly moved to Saskatoon. Harry Ornest took over as owner, pinched pennies, and never funded the Blues in a way that could surround Federko and Sutter with the necessary talent to push the team to a higher level on a consistent basis.

Still, Federko endured and kept controlling the puck, making those pretty passes, turning the likes of Mark Hunter into 40-goal scorers. With Federko leading the team in points 10 times in a 12-season stretch, the Blues remained respectable and popular and worthy of additional civic investment. The Blues eventually were stabilized by better ownership, and the historical contributions of Federko, Sutter and the Plagers should never be minimized.

The truth is, Bernie had plenty of reasons to be bitter. He came along too soon, and missed the big-budget era of Blues hockey. Underpaid as a player, he retired by the time NHL salaries started to escalate. The Blues and his old pal Sutter broke his heart by trading him to Detroit for his final NHL season. Then Federko had to wait, year after frustrating year, to gain approval from the Hall of Fame committee. As he kept getting shut out, Federko's emotional wounds deepened, but he resisted the urge to lash out. He reacted to each snub with admirable diplomacy.

In retirement, Federko ached to serve the franchise in a meaningful way. He wanted to be a general manager, or have a substantial role in shaping the Blues. He'd look around the league and see so many of his contemporaries running teams – former players such as Glen Sather, Mike Milbury, Doug Risebrough, etc. – and wonder why the chance eluded him. And friends say that even though Federko is happy in his role as the team's TV analyst, he still dreams of being involved in the hockey operation. Why? It's not his ego; it's his devotion. He desperately wants to help the franchise win a Stanley Cup.

This is such a wonderful moment for Bernie and the Blues. He is so loyal to the franchise. His abiding affection for the Blue Note has always been underrated. That loyalty truly separates him from so many other good players, and good men, who wore the uniform for a time as they passed through town. Bernie wanted to be here. He wanted St. Louis to be his home, always. He never wanted to leave. He never wanted to take the uniform off. He never wanted to do anything but serve and honor the Blues. No player has ever loved this franchise more than Bernie Federko. And now the No. 1 Blue is getting the love in return.

Mother's Day almost an unhappy one for the Prongers

BERNIE BIT • I'd gotten to know Chris Pronger pretty well by the time the Blues (stupidly) traded him. He was so green when the Blues acquired him from Hartford in the controversial deal for Brendan Shanahan, and it was interesting to watch him grow up in St. Louis. And by the way: After enduring this injury, and this scare, Pronger didn't miss a game. He was back on the ice when the series resumed in St. Louis, as if nothing happened. A baseball player would have missed two months.

DETROIT

"Would Mrs. Pronger please report to the ambulance, by the Zamboni? Would Mrs. Pronger please report to the ambulance?"

Can you imagine what that must be like? You are sitting in the stands, a proud mom, watching your son Chris Pronger play hockey for the St. Louis Blues. Suddenly your boy is felled by a wicked slap shot to the heart, and he collapses to the ice, and his eyes are rolling back, and his lips are turning purple, and he's unconscious, and his teammates are screaming for help, and the Detroit Red Wings are shouting for an ambulance, and all 19,983 fans in Joe Louis Arena have lost their voices, and the doctors are sliding across the ice to rush to his side, and they make an announcement over the public-address system, telling you to report to the ambulance, and you aren't sure if your boy is dying?

And it's Mother's Day.

"Would Mrs. Pronger please report to the ambulance, by the Zamboni? Would Mrs. Pronger please report to the ambulance?"

Elia Pronger and her husband, Jim, were there to see Chris captain the Blues to another victory, but instead they were being ushered to an ambulance, where he was strapped to a stretcher, his No. 44 sweater sliced open across the middle, so the doctors could attend to his heart.

Imagine what this must be like. Think of all the mornings of driving Chris to the rink to play pee-wee hockey, all those hours spent washing his hockey uniforms, all the days where he'd come home bruised and down in the dumps. Think of those exciting times when he became a star in junior hockey, the rush of pride when he was drafted second overall by the Hartford Whalers, the nights when his pro career was wobbling, and he'd call home to be cheered up. Think of the anxiety of the trade to St.

Louis, the anguish when the fans booed him there, and the satisfaction when he finally became a beloved star, named Blues team captain and appointed to a spot on Canada's Olympic hockey squad.

But now there's a stranger's voice on a loudspeaker telling you to come to an ambulance. A 23-year-old athlete, your son in the peak of his life, curled up, removed from his senses, not moving an inch? All of a sudden they're wheeling him off on a stretcher, and some Blues are praying, and some are crying, and they're holding hands to give each other strength. This could not be real.

Would Mrs. Pronger please report to the ambulance, by the Zamboni? Would Mrs. Pronger please report to the ambulance?

"Where's Chris?" Elia Pronger said, as she reached the arena basement. "Where's my Chris?"

She didn't know that Pronger had sent a message. Down on the ice, his left hand gripped the scruff of teammate Geoff Courtnall's neck. He pulled Courts close and said, "Tell my parents that I'm OK."

The Blues were comforted.

"That just shows you what a solid kid this is," teammate Kelly Chase said. "He's been knocked out, he's probably scared, but he knew his mum and dad would be upset, and he had the presence of mind to make sure they knew he was OK."

Elia Pronger was escorted to the ambulance, and climbed through the back doors to be with Chris. About two minutes later, she emerged, Jim beside her, and the Prongers got into a van with Blues general manager Larry Pleau, who drove them to Henry Ford Hospital.

We couldn't talk to Elia Pronger – no one wanted to bother her, anyway – but as soon as we saw the relieved look on her face, we knew that Chris would be fine.

Heck, by then Pronger was already raising cain with Blues trainer Ray Barile. "On the way to the hospital he was yelling at me to cut off his skates, and get his elbow pads off. He was being as ornery as ever," Barile said, smiling. "Before we left him at the hospital, he was complaining that he didn't want to spend the night there. It was like nothing had happened to him."

Pronger was put through some tests, and thank God, everything checked out. Pronger's heart, especially. He had taken a Dmitri Mironov slapper on the chest, and no one was sure if his heart had stopped beating. Pronger's heartbeat had slowed to an alarming rate, and he was in danger.

Pronger was doing well an hour after the episode, but when he lost consciousness, the worst kind of fear spread through Joe Louis Arena. Anyone who saw this in person was shaken, frightened. Were we all witnessing an unspeakable tragedy?

"He was turning purple," Courtnall said. "The doctors were massaging his heart. He looked scared. It just gave you such a sick feeling. You felt so helpless."

The medics were about to cart Pronger off on the stretcher, and that's when he grabbed Courtnall. The Blues were trailing 4–1 and would lose 6–1 in a playoff game that no longer mattered.

"He asked me how much time was left in the game," Courtnall said. "They were trying to get him out of there, but he kept saying, `No, no. Wait.' He wanted to get up and play. Amazing. I finally had to pull his hand off me so they could take him."

Pronger spent Sunday night in the hospital, his mom and dad by his side. This wasn't the best Mother's Day, but it could have been worse, much worse. It could have been the worst day in Elia Pronger's life, but she probably wasn't thinking about that when she kissed her son good night.

Hull arrives in Japan, stirring up patriotism, not controversy

BERNIE BIT • There is no question that The Golden Brett gets my vote as the most entertaining St. Louis athlete of the modern era. A goal-scoring machine, and a quote machine. The enemy of the goaltenders was a friend to the sportswriters. In terms of the publicity his mouth generated on a daily basis - some of it controversial - Hullie put the Blues at the top of the sports page, more than they'd ever been.

NAGANO, Japan

On his first day in the Orient, Brett Hull discussed patriotism, raw fish, karaoke, dorm-room life, bath houses, the global community, golf, his loyalty to Team USA, hanging out with athletes from the Virgin Islands and the true meaning of the Olympics.

It was a very good first day for the Golden Brett, the Team USA sniper from St. Louis. Hull did not insult anyone. He did not yap himself into any fresh controversies. He did not antagonize any humorless NHL officials. Hull even exchanged pleasantries with Tomas Sandstrom, the Swede who broke Hull's hand with a slash in a late-December game.

Hull was so red, white and blue on Tuesday that he should have been waving an American flag and twirling Fourth of July sparklers. Hullie came to Japan to make peace, not war. Hull as Madeleine Albright: let the diplomatic mission begin.

There were three possible explanations for his good conduct:

1. Jet lag. Hull was tired from the 13-hour flight to Tokyo.

2. The NHL ordered him to shut up.

3. He just got to Japan, and it's early. Give his famous oratory skills time to warm up.

Disappointed reporters expected Hull to be the hockey equivalent of Charles Barkley, who entertained us nightly with outlandish statements during the Barcelona Olympics in 1992.

"No way," said Hull, who was almost apologetic. "I know I have a reputation for being kind of obnoxious in the press. It's something I have to live with, but it doesn't mean I'm a bad guy."

"Hull was so red, white and blue that he should have been waving an American flag and twirling Fourth of July sparklers. Hullie came to Japan to make peace, not war. Hull as Madeline Albright: Let the diplomatic mission begin."

"I come here wide-eyed"

Hull pronounced himself thrilled to be an Olympian, happy to mingle with non-millionaire lugers and bobsledders, doing his part for international brotherhood. In his first stroll through the Olympic village, Hull was approached by athletes from Puerto Rico, the Virgin Islands, Canada and the United States, and he posed for photos. He also chatted with U.S. skier Tommy Moe and Canadian figure skater Elvis Stojko.

"I come here wide-eyed, hoping to gather everything in," Hull said. "I think it's awesome to be meeting so many of these people from different places on the globe.

"We're not here as NHL stars. We're here as members of the U.S. Olympic team. We're no different than any athletes from anyplace else. We just play in a league where we get paid lots of money. That's the only difference between us and a curler.

"It's a group of people together, trying to achieve the same things in different sports. They're all trying to do the best they can, and they're experiencing cultures that they're unfamiliar with. I think it's great to sit in the village and experience everything that there is."

Including the frothy Japanese beer. Asked if he knew any Japanese words, Hull joked, "Yeah – Kirin Light."

Hull expressed satisfaction with his rather spartan Olympic village accommodations. Unlike the elitist pro–basketball "Dream Teamers," who commuted from luxury hotels during their two Olympic stays, the NHL players are living with athletes from around the world in a dormitory–type setting that includes video–game machines, an Internet "surf" shop, a disco and a 24–hour cafeteria.

"I don't think I'd want it any other way," Hull said. "There's obviously a more comfortable way you could do it, but if you act like you're above everyone else, then you're not really being part of the Olympics. It would be a joke."

Hull is so worldly, in fact, that he said he doesn't view Team USA as a patriotic endeavor.

"I don't take it that far," he said. "I almost feel like I'm representing the athletic world. I'm representing St. Louis. I'm representing right wingers. I'm representing a lot of groups.

"It's just like everyone is coming up to us in the village and saying, 'Go, USA.' Even though you want the U.S. to win, you want to see everyone do well. Let the best athletes win."

"I like the love songs"

For now, Hull just wants to enjoy the experience. He is sharing a dorm room with Colorado Rockies forward Adam Deadmarsh, 22. Remarkably, Deadmarsh managed to fall asleep Monday night despite having Hull in the next bunk.

"I had to check him a couple of times during the night to make sure he wasn't dead," Hull said. "He was out. It was tough for me. I know in the NHL, guys have it put in their contracts that they get their own room, but I can't imagine not having someone to converse with."

The U.S. players are going to have a sushi (raw fish) lunch this week. "I like sushi," Hull said. "I want to see how they do it in Japan."

Team USA members also plan to try their voices in a Japanese karaoke bar – where patrons, accompanied by background music, sing on stage. "We have a lot of guys who think they can sing," Pat LaFontaine said. "Including Hullie. We'll find out."

Said Hull: "I'm not bad. I sound good."

And what will he sing? "I like the Bee Gees song, 'How Do You Mend a Broken Heart?'" Hull said. "I like the love songs."

First up, however, was a trip to a local golf pro shop.

"I have a note written in Japanese," Hull said. "It says, 'Dear Cabdriver, take me to the nearest golf store here.' Maybe I can bring some stuff home. Everyone knows I like golf better than hockey."

But the notorious Japanese bathhouses are declared off–limits. "I don't think it's something that many guys would go to, anyway," Hull said.

Canadians jeering Hull

Hull was pestered by Canadian reporters who once again pressed him on his U.S. citizenship – a sore subject in the 1996 World Cup, when the Canadian–born Hull (who has an American mother) led the victorious United States in scoring with seven goals.

"I'm still getting jeered in Canada," he said. "All I know is that I was a young guy without a career, and Team USA wanted me. What I do out on the ice, I do for a team that wanted me. Not to spite another team. I was born in Canada, but I'm a U.S. citizen. I'd rather be a guy who's loyal and thankful to the team that gave me a chance than go play for someone else. I'd much rather be a traitor, if that's what they want to call me."

Hull was in no mood to argue, however. Tuesday in the village, he bumped into Sandstrom, the Anaheim player who slashed Hull out of the Blues' lineup for five weeks. The two settled any remaining differences.

"He basically apologized," Hull said. "There are no hard feelings. I think he hit me on purpose, but I don't think he meant to break my hand."

Brett Hull at the Olympics: diplomat, Bee Gee and goal scorer.

We'll keep you posted, word by word.

Lessons are many in Keenan fiasco

BERNIE BIT • The night before the Blues officially hired Mike Keenan, I received an inside tip, met Keenan for dinner and was able to break the story that he was coming to St. Louis. At the dinner, I remember thinking that this was the guy who would lead the Blues to the Stanley Cup. I think a lot of us felt that way at the time. And we were wrong. Keenan's ego was too big for the city, and for the franchise.

> **"I** don't know if we characterize this as a failure, but it certainly was a learning experience for us."
> **– Blues chairman Jerry Ritter**

Yes sir, we all learned some lessons during our brief but educational relationship with Mike Keenan. Let's review:

• Blues fans discovered that they didn't want the name–brand coach with the driving, demanding and diabolical style. Oh, those tactics worked in other rinks for Keenan, who won in Philadelphia, Chicago and New York. But creative tension doesn't play too well in St. Louis, where the hockey players are treated as an adorable collection of "Tickle Me Elmo" dolls. Doesn't matter if the Blues are mediocre; many fans just want to be able to hug them. Keenan was doomed as soon as he traded his first pin–up boy, Brendan Shanahan. Keenan never got the message: The Blues are family. Don't mess with the family. Keenan failed to understand this sports community, and the loyalty it gives to familiar, pleasant athletes.

• Keenan learned that power can be intoxicating and dangerous. This was the role he coveted throughout his career: Master of The Universe. Keenan could wave his scepter and banish players, making them disappear before our eyes. He could – for no reason except to alleviate his own boredom – make a trade just to have some action. He could take the team to ski resorts for training. He could take a couple of days off in the middle of the season if he felt like it. As the madness escalated, he could build an escape door in his private office. He could take the team away from the public – sequestering the Blues in a private practice facility and cutting down on the number of community appearances that made the players so accessible and popular. Keenan had full control . . .

"Keenan never got the message: The Blues are family. Don't mess with the family. Keenan failed to understand this sports community, and the loyalty it gives to familiar, pleasant athletes."

but failed to control himself.

• We learned that Jack Quinn needed a conscience. The deposed Blues president, who did so many worthy things to grow hockey's popularity and status in St. Louis, pushed too hard and too far. The constant increase in ticket prices, the move to pay television and his "Let Keenan be Keenan" philosophy. Quinn is a superb sports executive, but, like many of us, he needed someone to whisper in his ear: Jack, back off. Don't do it. Bad move. Mike Shanahan played that role – the good cop to Quinn's bad cop – until he was ousted by the Kiel Center Partners. Someone had to sit on Quinn, and Quinn had to sit on Keenan. The system of checks and balances. But Keenan and Quinn together, unchecked, were trouble. Blood on the ice.

• We learned that Brett Hull won the power play with Keenan. One of them had to go, and the bosses fired Keenan. You don't see many professional sports teams siding with a player. But what will Brett do with this stunning victory? This is a great opportunity for Hull to exert his leadership in a positive, meaningful way. During this awkward transition, the Blues need him to be a great player and a dynamic presence. And if he starts pouting again, well, Brett will lose a lot of support. Hull says he cherishes the Blues, the fans and the city. Now he is in a position to prove it like never before. In the years he has left in hockey, Brett should strive to do everything he can to rejuvenate the Blues. Hull can't do it alone, of course. But he can make the most difference. I hope he understands the weight of his influence.

• Hopefully, the Kiel Center Partners learned that they know little about professional sports. They've taken the proper step here, taking the franchise back from Keenan. Now they need to sell the team. These men are giants in commerce, so shrewd and cunning in the corporate boardroom. But get them involved in the business of sports, and they're clueless.

Civilian businessmen can't impose their will on sports fans. Because fans invest as much emotion as money, any betrayal or loss of faith results in double the consequences. Even now, it's interesting to hear the KCP's reasons for whacking Keenan and Quinn. In his Thursday news conference, Blues Chairman Jerry Ritter rcpeatedly stressed the need for a fan-friendly approach. He emphasized the Blues' responsibility to make the fans happy, and to earn their trust.

This is all true. And we're not trying to pick on Ritter. He's a classy gentleman who is stuck in a difficult situation, having to front for the Kiel partners and members of Civic Progress. But don't these guys get it? They had those "fan-friendly" qualities in Mike Shanahan. And they removed him. The Kiel boys damaged their own business – rupturing a special relationship with the fans – to settle some petty, personal grievance with Shanahan. Too many rich guys were jealous of Shanahan, so they wanted to hurt him even if it meant hurting the Blues more.

What goes around, comes around. The new team president, Mark Sauer, is being hired to do for the Blues what Mark Lamping did for the Cardinals. And Lamping says Shanahan was his model when Lamping was hired by Anheuser-Busch late in 1994 to repair the fractured partnership with baseball fans. Isn't it ironic?

I suppose we all learned a valuable lesson: Be careful of what you wish for, because you might get it. We wanted Keenan. Until he got here. Then we wanted Keenan out.

Keenan was, and is, a brilliant hockey mind. But he was the wrong fit for the Blues and the community. There's plenty of blame to go around. Just wait. Many of the same fans who wanted Keenan's neck will be snarling at the new coach, 10 games into his employment.

Oh, well.

Being a Blues fan means never having to say you're happy. Will the curse of mediocrity ever be broken?

We move forward. We drop the puck.

And hope for better days.

The two faces of Gretzky show

BERNIE BIT • Wayne Gretzky is one of the greatest team athletes in sports history, but his time in St. Louis was strange and sad. Soon after an emotional Blues debut on home ice, in which he was moved to tears, Gretzky's mood changed. I never felt that he wanted to be here. He was aloof and above it all and gave me the vibe that he was just passing through town and couldn't wait to go.

The more I'm around professional sports, the less I understand people. Especially the athletes. Wayne Gretzky, for example.

Those No. 99 Blues jerseys soon will be collectors' items. Talks between the Blues and Gretzky have broken down. Gretzky has informed the Blues that he plans to test the free-agent market beginning July 1. We hear that the Phoenix Coyotes are making goo-goo eyes at Gretzky.

This isn't about money. I can't imagine that another NHL team will match the Blues' various proposals to Gretzky and his agent, Mike Barnett.

Initially, the Blues offered $23 million for three years. Gretzky hedged, and the Blues withdrew. The Blues then pitched a two-year deal for $12 million. Finally, the Blues restored the original three-year commitment but for fewer dollars ($15 million).

The Blues also offered Gretzky a small percentage of team ownership. Other sweeteners were included. A $1 million bonus if the Blues made the playoffs. Another bonus if the Blues won the Stanley Cup. A private luxury suite at Kiel Center for Gretzky's family. Free air travel for Gretzky's family.

That's a generous bounty for a 35-year-old center of declining – but still viable – skill. We can fault the Blues for yanking the $23 million offer from the table, but Gretzky-Barnett had that monster deal in front of them for two weeks and didn't sign. If Gretzky is sore at the Blues for lowering subsequent offers, well, he has only himself and Barnett to blame.

To repeat: Gretzky can help the Blues, even at inflated pay. If Gretzky can get a better deal elsewhere, more power to him. If he can't net a more lucrative deal from another team, that's his problem.

The Kiel Center Partners were willing to go to great lengths to retain Gretzky, but the Blues should stop their begging and move on. Spend the money on other, more grateful free agents.

What does Wayne Gretzky want?

Probably a kinder, gentler coach. Even if it means taking a pay cut.

Remember, Mike Keenan hollered at Gretzky after Game 2 of the Detroit playoff series. Keenan later apologized, but apparently failed to soothe Gretzky's feelings. Brett Hull has been saying it for months: Gretzky doesn't want to play for Keenan.

Gretzky has said so many things since he became a Blue, I don't know what to believe or what to dismiss. Is he genuine? Or is Gretzky just another phony athlete? What do we make now of Gretzky's kind comments about Blues fans and his fondness for St. Louis? Or his repeated desire to re-sign with the Blues.

Truth . . . or lies?

When the Blues acquired Gretzky from the Los Angeles Kings, he raved about Keenan. He said he wanted to play for Keenan. He said Keenan knew how to win a Stanley Cup, and Gretzky wants one more.

Surely, Gretzky was familiar with Keenan's methods before coming here. Hull – Gretzky's best friend in hockey – undoubtedly filled Wayne in. Keenan is tough to work for – but he also delivers his teams to the Stanley Cup finals.

Does Gretzky want special treatment? Should Keenan ignore flaws in Gretzky's play? In LA, the powerful Gretzky intimidated coaches. Will Gretzky permit any coach to challenge him? Is this a hockey player, or royalty?

Does Gretzky want to win a Cup? Does he still have the same relentless drive to win as, say, basketball's Michael Jordan? Or does Gretzky want a low-pressure gig in a sunny locale, surrounded by golf courses?

If so, it's time to reevaluate Gretzky. Or, for that matter, BOTH Wayne Gretzkys. There may be two.

There's the loyal Wayne who states his respect for Keenan and his affection for St. Louis and Blues fans. That Wayne wept when welcomed during his first home game at Kiel Center.

And then there's the mercenary Wayne, who turned his nose up when offered a generous pile of St. Louis money. That Wayne was criticized by Sports Illustrated when he deserted the Kings. I wrote a column in response, defending Gretzky's honor, and received an appreciative note from his agent.

Obviously, I didn't know Gretzky then. I don't know him now.

"There's the loyal Wayne who states ... his affection for St. Louis and Blues fans. And then there's the mercenary Wayne, who turned his nose up when offered a generous pile of St. Louis money."

Blues can take Sutter's job, not his heart

BERNIE BIT • In a perfect St. Louis sports world, the Blues would have won the Stanley Cup, and with Brian Sutter as coach. It's never easy when a coach is about to get fired, but this was especially hurtful, given all that Sutter had done for the franchise. The man loved the Blue Note and gave it everything he had. Sutter will always bleed blue.

Brian Sutter walked down a hallway, heading to the locker room, still coach of the Blues for now. A man in a tan suit stopped him, offering a handshake. A long-haired kid in a Blues jersey patted Sutter on the back, as he disappeared through double doors.

They knew. The Blues had just been bounced from playoffs by the Chicago Blackhawks. This abrupt first-round ejection took only six games, and we have probably seen the last of Sutter as the coach of this franchise. The 2–1 loss wasn't just the end of a tortuous season; it was the end of a bittersweet era. Sutter's eyes were a little watery, but the psycho glare still illuminated from his soul. The Blues can take away the job of his life, but no one gets the Sutter heart.

"The most competitive man I've ever known," Blues team captain Garth Butcher said. "He's meant more to hockey in this town than anybody, and to see him get beaten up really disgusts me."

Alone, Sutter sat down on a weight-machine bench. His head was down. A Sutter can cry. So can his wife, Judy, who waited for him outside, to gather up her man and take him home.

One question, and his emotions came pouring out. The same intensity that left more than a few enemy players stuck to the Plexiglas like bugs on a windshield in Sutter's days as a kamikaze left winger.

"When my family starts getting phone calls, saying that Brian Sutter shouldn't have a job coaching the Blues, it bothers me," he said of the criticism. "When my kids get calls, when they get people mouthing off to them about their father, you're darned right it bothers me.

"I know as a coach, I've got to be oblivious to it. I know what people have been saying about me, and I stay away from it. People can say what they want about me. It's part of the job. But when people start bringing my wife and kids into it, making them feel the pain, it hurts me a lot. I feel like I've been crucified."

The fans smell his blood, and they've gotten the scent from the top of the organization. Blues president Jack Quinn, who used to be Sutter's No. 1 patron, has backed away from his man. Quinn's low-key but blatant detachment tells us that Sutter is out of here. Team sources say the decision has already been made; a more kinder, gentler and flexible approach is deemed necessary for the Blues to grow.

Sutter isn't about to concede failure. "We've got a young hockey club," he said. "We're very young. We've undergone some major renovations. Our best days are ahead of us."

The irony: That young talent is the reason why Sutter probably will be terminated. Sutter likes bruises and welts. Losing teeth is preferred to making pretty plays. He has all this talent on his hands, but he's still preaching the old-time religion of blood and guts.

Sutter's critics say he treats young players as aliens. Because the prodigies are blessed with gifted hands and swift skating ability, the fire-breathing coach seems to assume that they don't care as much as the blue-collar Sutter clones. He grinds their confidence down to the nerve. (See: "Brind'Amour, Rod").

"Go in that room and ask those guys if they like playing for me," Sutter said. "People say I'm too hard on the players. If anything, I don't work them hard enough. Those guys played their hearts out for me tonight."

Sutter supervised a Blues team that suffered a 22-point drop from last season's 105-point tease, engineering most of the personnel moves himself. One fair question: Was this an off year for Sutter or the entire franchise? The Blues have been dysfunctional since losing defenseman/captain Scott Stevens in a botched arbitration ruling.

The turmoil has continued, uninterrupted: the retirements of Harold Snepsts and Rick Meagher, the Adam Oates soap opera, Brett Hull's childish pouting phase, the NHL strike. Is Sutter responsible for this commotion?

No. But the coach is responsible for motivation and fundamental precision. And too often this forgettable season the Blues have looked uninspired and disheveled.

And like most stubborn coaches who cling to a strong philosophical position, Sutter is viewed with contempt. Revisionist history has not been kind. Sutter is seen as a dinosaur who isn't pleased unless his players get bloody. This attitude once made him popular among the hard-core, working-class fans.

"No one wants to win more than I do," Sutter said. "Just remember that. I did the best I could."

Sutter got up. Assistant coach Wayne Thomas tried to console him. Sutter spun around, went off by himself. As a player and as a coach, a Sutter always goes into a corner alone.

"Sutter is seen as a dinosaur who isn't pleased unless his players get bloody.
This attitude once made him popular among the hard-core, working-class fans."

Hull, Oates make their magic count

BERNIE BIT • For a time, the Hull and Oates Show was the best in town. I wish we could turn back the clock and experience it again, because Blues hockey was never more exciting than those nights at The Old Barn, when Hull and Oates collaborated on ice.

We have seen the same scene of winter repeated so many times: The puck, momentarily owned by Adam Oates, is transferred to Brett Hull, who shoots to thrill with the most dangerous set of wrists in St. Louis since Stan Musial swung a bat.

Oates to Hull. A pass threaded, a snap of those killer hands, and then a blur so fast that the goalie might not be able to track it on slow-motion replay. The puck is DOA in the net. Turn on the red light. Strike up the Budweiser song. Another collaboration. Another goal. A new memory. We've been spoiled. The lightning bolts have become redundant.

But late in the second period last night at The Arena, Hull and Oates reminded us how extraordinary they are. That's when Oates passed to Hull to save the Blues' season. The latest goal, their greatest, came at a time when the Blues needed Oates to Hull like never before.

The hour was getting late in Game 7 of the Norris Division semifinals. The Detroit Red Wings had the audacity to show up and offer a contest. The Dread Wings of Game 1 were back, with Yzerman, Fedorov, Cheveldae and a vengeance.

The Red Wings were making 18,635 fans terribly nervous, tricking the Blues into a dump-and-chase house of mirrors. And to think that this would be easy. After all, the Red Wings had been driven to the rink in a bus that had a "Have A Nice Day" sign posted in the front window. Before the game, the Red Wings looked as wide-eyed as tourists from Iowa.

The Red Wings figured to be less threatening than a Bo Schembechler team in the Rose Bowl, but packed some composure into their garment bags for this trip after two successive losses that erased their 3–1 series lead.

And the Blues were tight. They couldn't get their forechecking game going, couldn't force the Red Wings into the usual giveaways, couldn't even bait Bob Probert into taking a dumb penalty. An Oakland Avenue freeze-out. Just what Detroit needed to pull off the shocker.

In the final minute of the second period, the Red Wings were feeling stronger and more confident, about to return to their locker room to plot the strategy that would end the Blues' season. The game was tied 1–1.

"If we go into the third period tied," Red Wings coach Bryan Murray said later, "then maybe there would have been some talk in the Blues' room that would have been disturbing."

And then . . .

Probert carried the puck down the left side, weighing options, looking to make a play in the Blues' zone. The Red Wings had a chance to score. If nothing else time would expire in the period, and the Blues' anxiety level would grow.

Oates slid over to cut Probert off, displaying the dexterity of a pickpocket. In a flash, the puck belonged to Oates – but only for an instant. Hull, as always, made a sneaky getaway. His destination was the Blues' bench.

"I was going to go off the ice," Hull said, "when I saw Adam get the puck. So I just turned and went up ice."

With his back to Hull, Oates gunned a backhand pass through the neutral zone. It was a pass made through telepathy, a pass seemingly made possible only if Oates has eyes in the back of his helmet. The Red Wings would call it blind luck. But Oates, see, always has eyes for Hull.

"As usual, Adam saw me," Hull said. "As usual, Adam made the play."

And so the puck was on Hull's blade, and he had two strides on the pursuing Yves Racine. They would race for the angle up the right side, sprint to the moment that would decide this series. Hull chugging forward, Racine catching up, Hull lurching ahead, Racine closing the gap.

Just when it appeared that Racine would win the speed–skating duel and drape enough of his body on Hull to prevent a hazardous shot, Hull got to a sweet spot in the right circle. Just enough room to let it rip.

Racine lunged. Too late. The wrists flexed. The puck flew. The blur appeared before Tim Cheveldae's eyes. What happened next was the Jack Clark home run in Dodger Stadium during the 1985 National League playoffs. The red light came on with 21 seconds remaining in the second period.

Oates to Hull. Lightning bolt. Budweiser song. Hull's eighth goal of the series, 94th of the National Hockey League season. Oates' ninth assist of the series, 99th of the season. A 2–1 lead for the Blues.

The Blues would score again after the break, riding the Oates-to-Hull momentum. Then the Blues would hold off the Red Wings for 18 pulsating minutes. The Red Wings came so close that the Blues needed to dial 911. But it ended 3–2.

The Hull goal stood. And so did the dream of a Stanley Cup. Oates to Hull, one chance, and the goal from nowhere. The biggest goal yet. The story of the season.

"... Pinkel went Dick Vermeil on us. The coach who improved his leadership and his relationships by softening his edges and sharing his emotions was at it again."

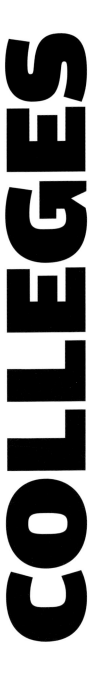

COLLEGES

Mizzou goes from old errors to new era

BERNIE BIT • I think back to all of those dreadful Saturdays in Columbia, and wondering if Mizzou would ever experience the joy of a triumphant football team. The dream finally came true. The 2007 season, a thrill ride, was capped on New Year's Day in Dallas.

"Chase Daniel and Tyler Luellen lifted Tony Temple and gave him a triumphant ride to the MU sideline. And that, my friends, was the scene that perfectly captured everything about this Mizzou team."

"Temple, a senior, knew what it was like to be a part of something special, to have made a difference in transforming a program. Heck, all of those MU seniors deserved a chariot ride off the field."

After his final gallop, which put him in the Cotton Bowl record books, which carried him into the end zone for his fourth touchdown of the game, Tony Temple finally stopped running. He grimaced in pain and hopped on his one good leg.

A tight hamstring was the only thing that could shut Temple down on this glorious day in Texas. The Arkansas defense couldn't do it. He was the Temple of doom for Arkansas, a Temple of zoom for the Missouri Tigers. Temple made so many hard-driving and nimble maneuvers, his legs finally gave out after 281 yards of daring, determined and destructive rushing.

And so now it was Missouri 38, Arkansas 7. This blowout was nearly complete, and Temple needed assistance. Hey, it's exhausting work to steal this Cotton Bowl away from Darren McFadden, the Arkansas super back. And so two teammates picked Temple up to bring him home. Quarterback Chase Daniel and tackle Tyler Luellen lifted Temple and gave him a triumphant ride to the MU sideline.

And that, my friends, was the scene that perfectly captured everything about this Mizzou team. They're talented. They're unselfish. They play for each other. It's all about team. Good players, good guys. It's what coach Gary Pinkel hoped to have at Mizzou one day, when he left Toledo to take a shot at rebuilding the Tigers.

Daniel didn't have a sharp passing day, so he happily handed the ball and the accolades to Temple. It was Daniel who gave Temple a hand up after the back's fourth touchdown.

"That's the definition of family," Temple said. "Our team is a family atmosphere out there. They don't want our guys to go down."

Once upon a time, we'd see Mizzou players hauled off the field under entirely different, and sadder, circumstances. They'd be limping and demoralized. All but ruined as competitors. Their sorry team would be losing by 31 instead of winning by 31.

This time, the injured player was smiling. Temple felt the joy of victory, the satisfaction of a 12-2 season that could promote Mizzou into the top five in the final polls. Temple, a senior, knew what it was like to be a part of something special, to have made a difference in transforming a program. Heck, all of those MU seniors deserved a chariot ride off the field after winning this game.

"The happiest thing for me was to see my players and coaches in the locker room just now, hugging each other and crying and holding on to each other," Pinkel said. "That's the most gratifying thing to me. I told them in the locker room after the game that this just didn't happen. We didn't wake up one day and say 'Hey, we're good.' It worked because we had kids who were committed, who had great attitudes, who worked hard, who became leaders."

Late in the game, senior tight end Martin Rucker had moved Pinkel to tears by reminding him of how far Mizzou had traveled over the past few seasons. "No one is laughing at us now," Rucker told Pinkel. "We're winners, Coach."

And Pinkel went Dick Vermeil on us. The coach who improved his leadership and his relationships by softening his edges and sharing his emotions was at it again.

"I was crying on the sideline," Pinkel said. "It's just overwhelming. What these players have done for Missouri football — and it's just not about Missouri football. It's about the University of Missouri. It's about the state of Missouri. It's about state pride.

"When I go around the state, recruiting and talking to folks and everything else, all the Mizzou fans are behind us. They're proud. And that was my vision someday, that everybody would embrace you. And they would be Missouri Tiger fans. We've come a long way, but this is just one chapter."

As he stood outside near the Mizzou locker room, feeling the winter wind and savoring the memories of this day, Pinkel thought about the beginning, when he took the Mizzou job in 2000.

"I had a number of coaches call me up," Pinkel said, "and ask, 'What are you doing? Why are you going there?' But I just felt, from the outside looking in, that it could be done. Everybody was talking about Missouri forever, and how you can't win at Missouri. But why can't you win at Missouri?"

You can, Gary. And you did.

Happy New Year.

Happy New Era.

There's no doubt: Snyder must go

BERNIE BIT • I've never believed it was the province of a sports columnist to call for the dismissal of a coach or manager. But the Tigers had reached the point of no return under Quin Snyder. At the beginning I thought he had it all; to this day, I still don't understand why he failed.

We're witnessing something of historic proportions: the most humiliating stretch of Missouri basketball in 40 years.

Quin Snyder's once-promising coaching regime has collapsed in the final weeks of his employment at Mizzou. The Tigers have lost six consecutive games by an average of 18.1 points. The futility is staggering.

Sure, there have been longer losing streaks. Norm Stewart-coached teams lost eight in a row in 1973-74, dropped seven consecutive games in 1978-79 and had another 0-7 skid as recently as 1992-1993. But those teams had pride and competed. Those players didn't quit on Stewart. They may have lost games, but many of the defeats were close. Unlike what we're watching now, there were no signs of surrender.

When Snyder arrived in Columbia, the hope and the belief were that he'd elevate the program by adding NCAA Tournament success onto Stewart's sturdy history of regular-season achievement. Instead, Snyder has taken the program back down to the level of Bob Vanatta in the mid-1960s. In his last two seasons as coach, Vanatta lost 43 of 49 games.

Obviously, Snyder's record over the last two years (26-28) isn't as hideous, but it can be argued that the embarrassment is just as severe, because the expectations were so high, and Snyder did manage to take the Tigers on a run to the NCAA Tournament's Elite Eight in 2002. But Mizzou basketball has been in steady decline since then.

Clearly, this team has quit on Snyder. We don't need to hear false testimony of players who insist they still want to play hard for their coach; our eyes can see the truth. A lazy, 90-64 loss to young but hungry Baylor was disgraceful. The Tigers barely offered resistance on the defensive end, the offense consisted of the usual pickup-game chaos, and temperamental players yapped at officials. It's a complete breakdown in all phases.

Tigers fans are ashamed of their program. And they're making it known at the box office; the Tigers are averaging only 8,200 fans at home. That's unthinkable, considering the extensive string of sellouts under Stewart, and the appeal of a new arena that was built to represent the new golden age of Mizzou basketball.

This must end. Now.

This is no different from a boxing match, where an overwhelmed fighter is so beaten down, bloodied and wobbled that it's cruel for him to continue and absorb more punishment. That's when the referee usually intervenes and stops the fight.

And Mizzou has reached that stage with Snyder.

I spoke to Missouri director of athletics Mike Alden. And though Alden was reserved and diplomatic in his comments, his frustration is obvious. Alden realizes that as long as he stays with Snyder, the more he'll be splattered with mud. The longer Alden sticks with Snyder, Alden puts his own reputation on the line. And more fans will be calling for Alden's ouster as well.

But Alden won't fire Snyder before season's end. According to Alden, Snyder will finish this one out.

"It's been my policy to let our coaches in all sports complete their seasons, and at the end of the season, we evaluate the performance,' Alden said. "We do that every season. And we'll do it this time."

Alden should make an exception in this case.

But if he won't, then Snyder should do the right thing and resign.

Snyder is gone at the end of the season, and surely he knows this. Just listen to his weekly radio show. On a recent show, host Mike Kelly asked Snyder how the coach planned to keep everyone up.

Snyder's response: "(Expletive), I'm down."

And that was before Mizzou got thumped by losses to Texas, Texas Tech and Baylor.

So what is the point of Snyder staying?

Short of a Norman Dale miracle, Snyder has no chance to keep his job – and this won't be a sequel to "Hoosiers." Most fans and alums have turned their backs on him, and the players don't care. Snyder's doomed status as their coach makes the situation worse. Until Snyder goes, he is the story, and the story won't go away, and the story is growing heavier and nastier by the day. This team has to be feeling the weight of Snyder's burden.

Each day that Snyder stays on is one less day that Mizzou has to start repairing the damage. And the sooner Snyder leaves, the sooner Mizzou can begin the healing process.

Snyder has been given every fair opportunity to succeed – from multiple contract extensions to a generous recruiting budget, to the new arena, to the support of a Mizzou administration hit with criticism for staying the course after the Ricky Clemons fiasco, NCAA violations, and official NCAA sanctions.

And now Snyder owes the university something in return: a letter of resignation.

Knight is back in Sweet 16 – without making changes

BERNIE BIT • For some reason, I qualified as one of the 25 or so sportswriters that Bob Knight liked. I always got along great with him - unless I'd ripped his pal, Tony La Russa. And then I'd hear about it. Knight was a great coach, and an American icon.

ALBUQUERQUE, N.M.

Texas Tech coach Bob Knight showed up for his news conference looking rather fresh and fashionable in a lavender sweater. What, does he have a new endorsement deal with Benetton? Even worse, Knight engaged in merriment with reporters, which certainly could be viewed as one of the seven signs of the apocalypse.

Who could predict that the Sweet 16 would give us the NutraSweet Knight? Surely, this will be interpreted as yet another sign that Knight is busy reinventing himself, evolving from old-school disciplinarian into a shining, new-age Knight.

Please.

Knight, 64, hasn't changed. It's become a trendy story line: Outdated coach is removed from his kingdom at Indiana, finds redemption in a backwater Texas town, becomes kinder and gentler, and suddenly re-emerges as a relevant figure.

Bob Knight guffaws at the theory that he's getting mushy after all these years. And he politely waves off suggestions that this season represents one of the best coaching jobs of his 39-season career.

"I haven't changed any," he said. "But all coaches have to work harder at teaching kids today than ever before because kids aren't nearly as grounded in fundamentals as they once were. But I don't sit here and analyze myself. What really concerns me is trying to figure out what flies I'm going to use next time I go fishing."

The fishing expedition is delayed. As Knight leads Texas Tech into the Sweet 16, understand that we're seeing a true giant of American sports in his element, proving that old-school methods still work.

The perceptions of Knight are all over the board. Those who dislike him always will view him as a bully. Those who respect him always will stress his attributes. Knight, meanwhile, isn't into image-making. He knows that the anti-Knight sides, and the pro-Knight sides, are entrenched.

And so is he. Knight still clings to the set of stubborn beliefs that were his foundation at Army and Indiana. He runs the motion offense, with players setting hard screens to create openings for shooters. He insists on playing gritty man-to-man defense. He demands toughness, intelligence, unselfishness and sound fundamentals. He enforces academic standards and graduates his players. And yes, Knight still occasionally vents his mind with howling gusts of political incorrectness. (Earlier this week, Knight went out of his way to demean Indiana coach Mike Davis.)

"To me, he's the same," said Cardinals manager Tony La Russa, a close friend who has known Knight since 1988. "He's a terrific competitor, he has tremendous knowledge of the game, and he's an excellent teacher. He must be awfully tough to coach against because his teams are so well-prepared. His system works. It never stopped working."

Indeed, this Texas Tech team reflects Knight's core values. Give him a hungry, coachable group of players who are willing to learn, willing to sacrifice, and he'll maximize their talent. Knight took over a lost-in-the-wilderness Texas Tech program four seasons ago, and he has led the Red Raiders to four 20-win seasons and three NCAA Tournaments. Knight can scoop up these basketball tumbleweeds and still make a team out of them.

Knight's reappearance in the Sweet 16 is being portrayed as a revival. And there's some truth in that, only because he had to start over after his dismissal from Indiana in 2000. But it isn't as if Knight's coaching suddenly has improved. In the latter years at Indiana, his recruiting declined, and that was the source of his teams' limitations. Knight pretty much got all that he could from those Indiana teams.

I asked Knight if the reports of his demise were greatly exaggerated.

"I don't know where our demise ever was," he said. "I think in the last (19) years we've been in the NCAA Tournament every year but once. And we've had teams that got into the tournament that probably had to give their last gasps of energy just to get in there. ...Those (Indiana) kids in my mind were really able to accomplish something that might have been thought of as being out of reach – just like these kids now."

Knight's friends have a different take. They're pleased that he's been vindicated.

"It pained all of us when he got criticized," La Russa said. "For a while the talent he had wasn't competitive enough. There was an opinion being expressed out there that the game had passed him by, and he wasn't the same coach. But if you give him an even chance with talent, he'll have a good team and he'll win."

Before the season, Texas Tech was picked to finish seventh in the Big 12 and miss the NCAA Tournament. Look at Knight now, among the remaining 16. Some say he's back. Truth is, he never went away.

Stewart deserves to be remembered as coaching giant

BERNIE BIT • My occasional feuding with Norm Stewart is my biggest regret as a sports columnist. I've tried to explain it this way: Norm could be an intimidating person, and as a young columnist, I had to stand up to him. But I went too far at times, a sign of immaturity, and I admit that. But things changed. In his final couple of seasons as coach, we got along well, and oddly enough, many of those who used to savage me for getting on Norm were now leading the wolfpack to oust him. I wish he could have had a happier ending.

Well, now Norm Stewart and Charlie Spoonhour can play a game . . . Shuffleboard, backgammon, checkers.

First, we heard the startling news that Spoon was retiring from coaching, cracking jokes as he bounced away from St. Louis University, headed for a cheeseburger in paradise.

Now comes a bigger shocker: Norm, at 64, apparently leaving his throne at Missouri after 32 seasons.

The circumstances of Stewart's departure remain uncertain. It depends on whom you talk with in Columbia. Two versions are making the rounds:

1. Stewart was pushed out by aggressive, ambitious athletic director Mike Alden and a university administration that's disturbed by the turmoil associated with the basketball program. Whether it's players transferring (was Keyon Dooling next?), Stewart losing patience with young players, Stewart's various feuds, Stewart's failures in the NCAA Tournament, or the fear of another NCAA investigation, the bosses concluded it was time to move on.

Stabilize. Energize. Mobilize. Find a coach who can win in March. If a young, charismatic coach such as Steve Alford could lead modestly talented Southwest Missouri State on a romp to the round of 16 in the NCAA Tournament, then what precisely was Missouri's excuse? Mizzou had the tradition, the reputation, the budget, an advantageous recruiting base. But in the past few seasons, Mizzou failed to win as many NCAA Tournament games as Southwest Missouri and St. Louis U. How could that be?

2. Stewart, who has a keen radar for politics, realized that his base of support was eroding. Prominent boosters and once-loyal fans shamefully turned on him. He figured it was a good time to settle up, pad his retirement fund and proceed to a stress-free life away from the spoiled athletes, ungrateful Missouri officials and the increasingly hostile gallery of critics.

Stewart, in his prime, wielded enormous power on the Missouri campus. Athletic directors, curators and other coaches feared him. That was no longer true. As the football program rebounded under the firm and classy leadership of Larry Smith, the balance of power shifted. Stewart lost the hammer.

When Missouri's search committee interviewed Alden for the job, he was asked, point-blank: If firing Norm Stewart was the right move to make for the university, would you do it?

Alden's answer: Absolutely.

Alden was hired virtually on the spot.

Stewart saw what was coming, sooner or later.

The timing of this switch is a bit unusual only because Stewart had revived the Tigers during the 1998-99 season. He improved his recruiting and steered a youthful team back into the NCAA Tournament. The immediate future, if not radiant, was at least bright. At least he went out on a successful season.

I hope that the resignation was voluntary, because Stewart deserved to depart on civil terms. He was, and is, a giant in this state. Stewart not only put Missouri basketball on the map, he gave it color and life and distinction.

Norm won 634 games at Mizzou, emerged as a consistent conference force, took 16 teams to the NCAA Tournament, packed the Hearnes Center, made money for the school. The Tigers became a source of pride for the entire state. Stewart's work was so significant that the Mizzou coaching job is now one of the most appealing situations in the nation.

In my 20-plus years of sportswriting, Stewart was the toughest, most resilient competitor I've seen at the coaching level. He could freeze a room with his glare. His personality could dominate an arena. You could see other coaches, game officials and VIPs shrink in his presence. Stewart beat cancer, overcame NCAA probation and outlasted most of the rival coaches who were supposed to take him down. A piece of his heart went into all 634 victories.

He was never dull. Stewart was, and is, a truly fascinating character. A complex man. A compelling man. A controversial man. A man of contradictions.

* He could dominate the Big Eight, dominate the region, and approach his job with supreme confidence ... only to become unsure of himself in the NCAA Tournament, where he frequently stumbled.

* He could handle the life-threatening cancer with extraordinary grace and courage ... only to snap and boil over in a silly overreaction to an insignificant irritation.

* His fighting spirit appealed to the underdog in all of us ... but he could be cruel to the so-called little guys – the powerless underlings who worked for him or otherwise crossed his path.

* He has a wonderful sense of humor, personal warmth ... but could turn cold and vicious in an instant.

* He'd coach against Kansas or some other blood rival with all the

"Stewart was the toughest, most resilient competitor I've seen at the coaching level. He could freeze a room with his glare. His personality could dominate an arena."

passion and controlled fury that he could muster, willing his team to victory . . . but take an indifferent approach in other conference games, sitting on the bench in a catatonic coaching state.

His entire career, in a sense, was a contradiction: Norm Stewart is probably the best college basketball coach never to reach the Final Four.

That should not be his coaching epitaph.

Rather it should say he took a program out of the ashes and turned it into something special. He gave Missouri an identity that has endured for 32 years. And Mizzou basketball will continue to thrive because of the formidable foundation he established. That's more important, more lasting, than a fleeting moment in the Final Four.

Long may you storm, Norm.

It was a loss for the ages, but a win in our hearts

BERNIE BIT • I'm not one for moral victories. But I don't think I've ever been as proud of a team in defeat as I was with this Mizzou football squad. They deserved so much better that day. I think members of that team can look back with pride, knowing that they played a role in turning the program around.

COLUMBIA, Mo.

The Missouri Tigers were stunned, aching in ways that we never will comprehend. They had played the game of their lives, against the No. 1 team in the nation, and they deserved to win, but were denied by a set of Nebraska fingertips.

"It was like someone had reached in," senior nose tackle Donnell Jones said, "and ripped our hearts out. I've never felt so much pain." After a 45-38 overtime loss to Nebraska, Missouri's faith in many things was shaken, but these players still believed in God. So one by one, inside their hushed locker room, they dropped to their knees, put their heads down, and prayed.

"We thanked the Lord for allowing us to play this game," senior tailback Brock Olivo said. "And for keeping us healthy and for watching over those of us who were injured."

For a long time, this was the only sound in the locker room: the low whispers of a mournful college football team, seeking solace and strength from the heavens.

"I was shocked," Olivo said. "No one could talk. No one could look at each other without breaking down. It was like a morgue. It was like a funeral. Everyone was crying. It was total heartbreak. Shock. Disbelief. Did this really happen to us?"

It really happened.

Missouri, up 38-31, had its miracle secured. On the final play of the fourth quarter, the Tigers had gotten in the way of a last-second pass thrown by Nebraska quarterback Scott Frost. Mobs were poised to storm Faurot Field and rip down the goal posts.

And now, suddenly, in the tumbling chaos of falling bodies, dangling legs and waving arms, the football was deflected and kept alive in the north end zone. That tantalizing football hung in the crisp night air for an extra second, defying gravity, denying Missouri, dashing the dreams of underdogs, everywhere.

Floating . . . teasing . . . the ball. Get the ball. Someone in a Missouri uniform just had to swat that ball. But the ball stayed up. That extra second of agonizing suspension was sufficient to turn Mizzou's incredibly uplifting win into a cruel, crushing, stomach-flipping disaster.

Just at the bottom of the "O" in the sequence of letters that spells out Missouri, Nebraska split end Matt Davison reached for the football and plucked it with his fingertips, just before the ball skimmed the top of the grass.

Touchdown, Nebraska. No time left on the clock. The game was tied, overtime commenced, and the unbroken, unmerciful and still undefeated Cornhuskers zoomed in for a quick kill. The Tigers walked off the field, appearing to have been pierced with a shot fired by a tranquilizer gun.

That deflected pass. Davison's grab. The moment that dropped hearts across the state. It happened at the "O." Right there. The same end zone where Colorado scored on the infamous fifth-down play in 1990. Right at the "O."

As in: OH, NO!

Matt Davison as Tyus Edney.

Different sport, same lightning bolt.

Is it fair?

Nebraska has won a bazillion games since the Tigers last felled them in 1978. Mizzou has been down and out and off the college-football radar screen for 13 seasons, until this year's splendid ascension. Saturday at Far-Out Field, Mizzou's flash-dancing quarterback, Corby Jones, had Nebraska's mighty red army on the run.

The Tigers were announcing to the rest of the nation: Hello, again. We're back. The lost colony of college football has returned, and we'll show you. Yes, toppling No. 1 would have been the symbolic crowning achievement in this comeback season.

In this quest, Mizzou was fearless and fantastic. "Our game plan was very simple," coach Larry Smith said. "Go right after them. It was a run, hit and tackle game. That's all it was."

Missouri had bloodied the bully in red, getting the best of a memorable day of football combat. And then, in the north end zone, right at the "O," the football was up into the air . . . it struck a foot, maybe a shoe . . . up in the air, rotating and spinning, waiting to be claimed.

Nebraska didn't need this. Nebraska didn't need this as much as Missouri, and Mizzou fans, needed this. In a flash, Davison was there, finding the magic cornstalk in the grass in the north end zone. Right at the "O."

Oh, no.

Some day, after they shake off the grief, these players will know that they warmed hearts from Kansas City to St. Louis and all places in between. They will know that when they went down in this bitter defeat, the state drooped with them.

Their courage in going for Nebraska's throat was inspirational. And the way they lost . . . well, if you bleed anything but Nebraska red, you had to feel hollow inside.

Smith described the Mizzou locker-room scene as "total devastation. Those players left everything on the field. There's nothing left. I couldn't be any prouder of them in a victory. We'll have to get their heads back up, but we can't bounce back tonight. There's a lot of crying going on."

The Missouri players gathered for their postgame prayer, then there was more silence. Coach Smith moved to the center of the locker room.

"Coach was kind of speechless," Olivo said.

Finally, Larry Smith spoke to his team.

"He told us that he was damned proud of us," Olivo said, probably not realizing that his coach had spoken for all of those who care about Missouri's valiant football team.

Hightower earns his stripes with sheer diplomacy

BERNIE BIT • For years I watched Ed Hightower work the floor as one of the top college basketball officials in America. And I always thought that, in terms of performance, Hightower was the best person on the court. Better than the players, better than the coaches — he was just a model of excellence and consistency. I got to know Ed, and we became friends, and that's how this column came about. I just wanted to see how he prepared for a game, and how he ran it. How he trained his mind and body.

ON THE ROAD (with America's best college basketball official)

It's 9:35 a.m on a Sunday, and Ed Hightower is surrounded. We've just pulled into a Budgetel in Effingham, Ill., to pick up a new passenger.

Dave Elson, the superintendent of Litchfield (Ill.) schools, slides into the back seat. He is wearing a red, Bob Knight-replica Indiana sweater. This would indicate a strong rooting preference for Sunday's heated, blood-feud showdown between state rivals Purdue and Indiana in Bloomington. Another Hoosier fan and Hightower friend, Larry Thompson, is driving Ed's Lincoln for the trip to Bob Knight's lair at Assembly Hall. Thompson, a retired educator who taught Hightower biology in high school, also is draped in IU clothing.

There is no way out for Ed Hightower, a prisoner in his own automobile. Two Indiana basketball fans and a sportswriter are loaded in, and he's about to be heckled for the first time today.

"Going to be a close game, Ed," Elson chirps. "Might need a call from you."

"Ed, I thought you missed a couple last week when Indiana lost at Michigan," Thompson tells him.

Hightower smiles; he enjoys being razzed by his buddies. But then, just a hint of the official comes out . . .

"No complaining," Hightower announces. "I don't want to hear it. If I do my job, hopefully both teams will be in a position to play their best and have a chance to win."

Friendly, but serious. The essence of Ed Hightower, an esteemed judicial presence who has worked seven Final Fours and four NCAA national championship games in the past decade.

When it's a big game, you want Hightower in the black and white stripes. He is so graceful out on the court, so controlled and dignified, he should be wearing a tuxedo. He's been running miles in those Division I gyms for 17 years and has rejected several offers to officiate in the National Basketball Association.

This is how a working day in the life of Hightower begins. We departed at 8 a.m. from a restaurant parking lot in his hometown of Alton. We will drive 200-plus miles to Bloomington. We will watch Hightower officiate a beautifully played Purdue-IU game, televised nationally by CBS. We will go behind the scenes to see what he goes through – and what he thinks – as he prepares to dispense basketball justice in a fair manner.

We will see him nurse an injury. We will see him pacify Knight and Purdue coach Gene Keady, prevent a skirmish between players. And then we will drive back to Alton — guided out of Bloomington in grand style, by a traffic-busting police escort.

Rest Stop

Hightower does 50 games each season; that's down from 65 in his peak years. For 13 years, he was the acclaimed principal at Eunice Smith Elementary School in Alton. For the past two years, he's been the assistant superintendent of Alton schools.

Hightower also is working on his doctorate, taking classes at St. Louis U. And then there is his wife, Barbara, and their daughters, Julie (18) and Jennifer (13).

It's a hectic schedule, and Hightower is a meticulous planner. He logs his schedule in a black book, and his daughters know where to find it.

"The girls will have something planned for me," Hightower said. "Julie had a senior night at school. So she wrote in my book, under the date, `DON'T SCHEDULE ANYTHING.' That way, I know."

The routine is a grind. Thursday night, Hightower did the Cincinnati-Louisville game. Saturday afternoon, Hightower was in Peoria for Bradley-Illinois State. Then it was Bloomington on Sunday. Monday night, he zipped into Lawrence for the Missouri-Kansas rematch. Four games in five days.

This is why, an hour outside of Bloomington, Hightower fades from the conversation, gently puts his head back, and snoozes.

Game Plan

After some splendid, James Bond-caliber stunt driving by Larry Thompson through the back roads of southern Indiana, we wheel into the parking lot at Assembly Hall.

Hightower flies to about half the games on a private plane. A pilot friend delivers him through the air, saving a lot of time, getting Hightower back home a few hours after the game. When he drives, Thompson usually helps.

Outside the gym, Hightower is immediately recognized by Indiana fans.

He is treated like a visiting celebrity.

Hightower, 44, has come a long way from those muggy nights in the gym at SIU-Edwardsville, when he was paid $1.25 to ref intramural games.

"I learned if I could take the heat from those fraternity brothers," Hightower said, "I could handle anything."

Hightower likes to arrive about two hours before tipoff. Why so early?

"I go in and relax, get a flavor for what kind of game it's going to be," he said. "One hour before we start, I sit down with my crew and discuss the game. We form our own scouting report. Every game has a different makeup. So we talk about what to expect."

And Purdue-Indiana?

"Today, we have two teams from the same state, and this will be an intense, emotional game," he said. "As officials, we'll need to talk about how we can't go out there and be all emotional. The coaches and the players will be on edge, the fans will be a little goofy.

"I should be predictable. I should be the one person in that arena who will maintain a cool head, be reliable. That's my responsibility. Calmness."

Soon enough, Hightower's pregame concerns will materialize, testing his ability to mediate. He will prevent the crucible at Assembly Hall from bubbling over.

A Time For Solitude

Fifteen minutes before tipoff, Hightower and partners Randy Drury and Verl Sell are about to evacuate their sanctuary. It's the locker room normally used by IU's wrestling team.

First, Hightower has something to do. He finds a quiet corner.

"I always say a little prayer," he said. "Give me the wisdom. Give me the judgment. Give me the knowledge."

Game time, and 17,371 red-dressed fans buzz with anticipation in this divine cathedral of college basketball. The Indiana band goes wild, blaring the school fight song as cheerleaders tumble, prance and dance.

"I love these games," Hightower said. "The colorful atmosphere, the strategy by great coaches, the talented players. When those individuals do what they do best, it's like going to a musical to hear a wonderful singer. Or going to a museum to see a Picasso. It's art."

Hightower said his blood rushed as he stepped onto the floor moments before game time, as he felt the heat of the bright arena lights on his neck.

Keeping The Peace

Loose ball.

Purdue's Herb Dove and Indiana's Richard Mandeville get locked up. They jostle, point fingers. Dove is pulled away by teammates, but he hollers at Mandeville. The fans scream. This could get ugly.

Hightower takes control. This is the situation he envisioned before the game, a sudden eruption of emotion.

He calls the players together, tells them to settle down. He warns them that he will tolerate no more confrontations. Mandeville and Dove shake hands. There are no more incidents. Later, Dove approaches Hightower and apologizes for losing his cool.

"I try to work with them. I have a nice rapport with the players," Hightower said. "They know I'm going to talk to them, do what I can to keep them in the game."

Hightower has called only two technicals all season. Knight and Keady snarl in his direction a few times Sunday, but nothing major. Hightower wants coaches to vent — as long as the hot air doesn't interrupt the flow of the game. So Hightower takes no offense when Keady informs him that the official needs a vision test.

No harm, no (technical) foul.

"Any official who has to rely on technical fouls to control a game is an insecure individual," Hightower said.

The Getaway

Purdue's Chad Austin has just hushed the fretting Indiana faithful with a 3-point bomb, giving the seventh-ranked Boilermakers a 74-72 victory with 13.7 seconds remaining.

Forty-five minutes after the game, traffic still knots the access roads to Assembly Hall. Bloomington police offer to provide some open-road blocking.

Suddenly, we're following the flashing lights of a police cruiser. Traffic is halted; a path is cleared. We zoom up the middle of the street past hundreds of cars, Thompson straddling the center line.

We roll through two red lights. No intersection can stop us. We avoid a 30-minute jam. We're out of Bloomington in two minutes. Hightower salutes the policeman as we pull onto State Road 46, with nothing but open asphalt before us.

Before long, Hightower has a pulsating gizmo hooked up to his left calf. He tore the calf muscle last season, and the scar tissue occasionally flares up. So Hightower goes to the doctor for treatment at 6:30 each morning. He travels with an electronic stimulator that he straps on to soothe the calf muscle.

We reach Alton at 8 p.m., but Hightower still has another assignment. He sits down in his home office to review the tape of the Purdue-Indiana game. He makes notes, grades his performance.

Understand that no one is harder on Ed Hightower than Ed Hightower.

"You work to get respect, develop a good reputation," he said. "And it can all vanish in a moment if you forget what got you there."

MU throbs with pain after heroic effort

BERNIE BIT • I'll never forget that vision of seeing Tyus Edney streaking up the court, and thinking, 'There's no way he can get there on time.' But he did. Edney not only crushed the spirit of the proud Tigers, but UCLA proceeded to win the national championship. The course of history was altered in those 4.8 seconds.

BOISE, Idaho

UCLA's Charles O'Bannon interrupted his pleasure to seek out an old friend in need. Missouri's Jason Sutherland was in agony, down on his knees, pounding the floor and staring up at the ceiling, asking himself why, oh why, did this happen?

O'Bannon grabbed Sutherland by the shoulders and gently pulled him up. O'Bannon hugged Sutherland.

UCLA's 75-74 victory was so excruciating in its suddenness that the triumphant victors felt a moral obligation to console the valiant losers.

Three summers ago, when Sutherland and O'Bannon were hot-shot high school stars, they shared a room at a summer basketball camp and became instant pals.

"But back then," O'Bannon said, "you don't really imagine playing a game like this."

A streaking flash of lightning — bearing a strong resemblance to UCLA point guard Tyus Edney — had just passed through the Missouri defense, leaving it numb. Edney's game-winning runner in the lane wormed through the net as the buzzer sounded, and the Mizzou players fell as if struck by the thunderbolt.

So all over the court at the Boise State University Fieldhouse, UCLA players helped the Missouri players restart their heartbeats, regain their balance. It was a wonderful display of mercy and appreciation, compassion and respect. An acknowledgment of sharing in something special.

"Man, those guys from Missouri played hard," UCLA senior Ed O'Bannon said. "I mean, REALLY hard. They weren't going to give us anything for free, and that's the way it should be."

UCLA and Missouri were a reminder of why we invest our emotions into sports. It was a beautiful basketball game, a spectacle, a privilege to watch. One day the Mizzou players will feel a warm rush for having participated in it. But not now.

"I don't know what the Missouri players are feeling," Charles O'Bannon said. "But I feel terrible for them. All I could do was hug Jason Sutherland. I didn't know what to say to him."

With 4.8 seconds left, Mizzou's Julian Winfield had finished off a remarkably poised and perfect pass from hard-charging freshman Kendrick Moore, banking in the gimme layup that put the Tigers ahead 74-73.

In the final 10 minutes the teams had furiously clawed at each other, the lead changing hands eight times as every throat in the arena tightened.

"It was," Ed O'Bannon said, "the most intense game I've ever been involved in. They gave us their best shot, and we gave them our best shot."

And in the next-to-last shot, Winfield had put the 23rd-ranked Tigers on the verge of a shocking upset over the No. 1 Bruins.

Still, there was time for another gasp. UCLA called a timeout.

As the teams emerged from the huddle, Mizzou coach Norm Stewart stared at the court, then momentarily covered his face with his hands. The tension was extreme. The building seemed so humid. Who turned on the heat? How could something be so great and so horrible at the same time?

Everyone in the place knew what would happen next: the ball and the game would be handed over to Edney, who has the kind of speed you'd normally see blazing out of UCLA's football backfield.

"We wanted to give Tyus the ball and just get out of his way," Ed O'Bannon said. "Unless he needed us."

Edney would do this by himself, thanks, trucking about 90 feet in four scintillating seconds. Mizzou — in an inexplicable defensive gaffe that will haunt the team all summer — never picked Edney up. Mizzou gave him the fast lane. Invited Edney to be a hero. The court was Edney's own private Idaho.

Edney kept going . . . left side . . . around Sutherland . . . into the lane . . . veering right . . . the berserk Edney wasn't going to stop until he delivered UCLA to the West Regional in Oakland.

Help!

Someone wearing the Mizzou gold had to step out, slow the speed racer down. But Stewart had warned his players: don't foul. Whatever you do, boys, don't foul. So the Tigers were in a state of defensive paralysis as Edney zoomed by them.

Incredible, that Missouri's grinding, resilient season would end with such little resistance. The Tigers had overcome so much: the loss of eight players from last season's Elite Eight team, the depressing exit of sophomore sensation Kelly Thames because of a preseason knee injury, Winfield's late-season breakdown, the untimely February slump.

But the Tigers were still up. On their feet. By a point. And if Mizzou could suck in the oxygen one more time, and make a defensive stop, it would advance to the Sweet 16. No one expected that. Not after last season, not before this season, not now. But someone had to turn Edney back. Someone had to perform some heavy labor, one more time.

Edney darted inside. At the last instant, Grimm raised his hands in a desperate attempt at interference, but Edney's shot kissed the glass and fell true.

"This is the sweetest," Edney said. "The greatest shot I can think of. The greatest shot of my life."

Just like that, Mizzou's unlikely march — and March — was over. The Tigers, devastated, seemingly needed only 4.8 seconds to evacuate the arena. They did not even pause to shower. They would take their sweat, and their tears, onto the bus, to be alone in their misery.

Before heading out into the dusk, the players formed a tight little circle in the locker room. Sutherland and Paul O'Liney, Chip Walther and Corey Tate, the Haley Twins and Thames in street clothes. All of them sitting down, heads drooping, too removed from their senses to speak.

"We just lost," Sammie Haley said. "Can't you give us some time?"

Time.

If only Missouri could get those 4.8 seconds back.

Billikens tap big crowd's energy source

BERNIE BIT • Oh, happy days. Through the decades, Billikens fans haven't had much to cheer about, but this was a sweet time. The Spoonball Era, with the success and capacity crowds, showed that big things were indeed possible for SLU basketball.

It wasn't a basketball game; this was Spoonball's unofficial coming-out party. Mayor Freeman Bosley Jr. was in the house, on his feet and clapping for every St. Louis University basket.

Cardinals manager Joe Torre phoned Charlie Spoonhour and asked for tickets. Torre even donned headsets so he could chit-chat at halftime on the SLU radio broadcast. "I figured I'd better give Torre tickets," Spoonhour said. "Chances are I'll need some during baseball season."

Spoonhour is the No. 1 Cardinals fan. Now, the Cardinals are coming to watch his team play. Cardinals outfielder Bernard Gilkey sat behind the St. Louis U. bench and enjoyed himself.

Former Billikens star Monroe Douglass was in the stands, proud to be an alum. Philadelphia Phillies outfielder Milt Thompson checked in to root for SLU.

There was a Who's Who of high school coaches from around the city and region, led by Vashon's Floyd Irons. A potential Billikens recruit, St. Charles West guard Ryan Robertson, stood and cheered for SLU.

Didn't see Norm Stewart, though.

But just about everyone else was present and accounted for. Or so it seemed. A record crowd of 18,073 filled every cobwebbed corner of The Arena on Tuesday night to watch SLU thrash Memphis State 86-59.

Memphis State is taller, quicker, more established. Didn't matter. The Billikens have tapped into something special. The overflow crowd is an energy source.

"That was a great atmosphere," senior Donnie Dobbs said. "It makes you want to play harder, give all you've got. I love hearing a big crowd ranting and raving."

If you enjoy team basketball, the Billikens are a delight. They're unselfish. No one cares about individual stats. Ten players scored against Memphis.

Guard H Waldman was omnipresent. Center Evan Pedersen threw his body on loose balls. The defense forced 19 turnovers — 14 on steals

— and made it difficult for Memphis State to lob inside to big man David Vaughn.

This short SLU team can't even dunk — only two slams all season — but they pass until finding an open man who has a clean look at the basket. Waldman, Erwin Claggett and Scott Highmark blistered the nets for 3-pointers.

The lead reached 32 points. Spoonhour packed the fans in; his players sent them home early. The Billikens ran the Tigers from here to Graceland and back, improving to 13-0.

This is wild. SLU . . . unbeaten in mid-January . . . 18,000 zanies squeezed in . . . the celebrities flocking to courtside . . . on a Tuesday night . . . and Brett Hull ain't playing.

Evan Pedersen is getting standing ovations? Isn't this supposed to be a hockey town?

"This is beautiful," Claggett said. "To see a crowd like that, words can't describe it. It's something that SLU hasn't seen for a long time. For us to get that kind of support from the city of St. Louis is something that really makes us feel great."

In the 78 years of St. Louis U. basketball, never have so many people turned out for a home game. And never have so many jumped on the bandwagon. Hey, everyone is welcome. It's not too late. The VIPs are filing in to join the fun.

"The mayor was here? Cool," Claggett said.

The Boz departed with 3 minutes remaining, and SLU rolling along like an approved sales-tax measure, 80-49. "We're in good shape," Bosley said. This is different than the annual, pre-Christmas Missouri-Illinois assembly, which is divided in loyalty. The St. Louis U. audience is pure St. Louis. And this city has caught the fever.

The only holdouts are some petty St. Louis-based Mizzou fans, who hate seeing another state program prosper. Too bad. Let them stew. There's enough good basketball to go around. Everyone should relax and enjoy the accomplishments of both teams.

"I'd like to play Missouri," Claggett said.

And who would win?

"St. Louis University, of course," Claggett said.

Final score?

"St. Louis 100, Missouri 0," Claggett said.

Uh, guess again.

But what's wrong with sending a little trash talk west on Interstate 70? This is a giddy time for SLU. Gov. Carnahan better call for tickets soon, or he'll be left out.

A Christmas classic: Miracle on Oakland Ave.

BERNIE BIT • I wish I had a video copy of this unbelievable game, so I could relive it from the calm and comfort of my living room. Sitting at courtside, I thought my head was going to implode from the combination of deadline pressure, and the crazy twists and turns of an epic struggle.

If required, Missouri and Illinois were determined to play until Christmas morning to settle this. No surrender. No holiday curfew.

Just play on until they — or the ancient Arena foundation — couldn't stand the force of another wiped-out body tumbling to the ground. One more minute of madness, and we'd all collapse. They sparred for 40 physical minutes, simply refusing to melt like the snow flurries outside. Two valiant teams spilled into one overtime, then carried their drama onto a second OT, then dragged themselves into a third.

Do we dare go for a fourth?

Midnight, anyone?

"That one will go down in Missouri history," Tigers forward Jevon Crudup said.

In the Miracle on Oakland Avenue, Missouri survived, somehow outlasting No. 19 Illinois 108-107 despite having five players foul out.

At the end, Mizzou coach Norm Stewart prevailed with a patchwork lineup of Kelly Thames, Jason Sutherland, Derek Grimm, Lamont Frazier and a hobbled Reggie Smith on the floor.

"We've got the sick and the wounded playing," Stewart said. "Women and children were next."

The Illini were dejected but couldn't stay depressed for long. They knew that they'd participated in a classic. They knew they'd helped create a free-form masterpiece for the crowd of 18,273.

"A game like this was great for college basketball," Illinois coach Lou Henson said. "It was really an honor to be a part of."

It was three hours of delight and spent passion. The fireworks were enough to blow the doors off the old barn, which may never house this precious rivalry again.

"They'd start out on us; we had to fight back," Frazier said. "And before you knew it, it was onto the next overtime."

The players just had to be consumed, dazed by the intense emotion

"The players just had to be consumed, dazed by the intense emotion that flowed out of them. ... Mizzou and Illinois exchanged elbows, key shots, comebacks, heartache, exuberance and theatrics."

that flowed out of them. "You can't feel tired in overtime," Frazier said. "If you're trying to win, you just have to dig deeper."

Thanks for digging so deep. Thanks for the memories of a wicked Wednesday evening. Mizzou and Illinois exchanged elbows, key shots, comebacks, heartache, exuberance and theatrics.

What a resilient performance by underdog Missouri. The Tigers had labored to beat the mice on their schedule. The Illini figured to roll. But this is when Stewart is most dangerous — when you underestimate him.

Almost by script, the shaky Tigers blew a 13-point lead in the second half. Mizzou seemed doomed when Illinois took command 74-65 with less than two minutes remaining in regulation.

Missouri came back . . . again and again. Flailing away, bombing 3-point shots, refusing to go away. Super pests, with batteries that wouldn't expire.

Illinois missed 19 free throws; seemed like a thousand. You had to feel for freshman point guard Kiwane Garris, who slashed for 31 points but couldn't come out of this as the hero.

At the end of the second OT, the game was tied at 97-97. No time on the clock. Garris, fouled, stared at the basket, about to attempt two free throws. He hits one, the Illini win.

"I figured the game was over," teammate Richard Keene said.

The eyes of two states were upon young Garris. The Arena squeezed tighter, getting smaller and uncomfortable.

Garris missed the first. Teammate T.J. Wheeler, circled behind him and looked up into the stands, smiling. This was crazy, wasn't it? Maybe a once-in-a-lifetime game.

Garris cocked to shoot again. Clank. His heart sank. Garris will win many games for the Illini, but not this one. The Mizzou bench erupted. The Tigers seized the momentum in the third OT.

"Garris played so hard, gave us everything he had," Henson said. "I'm proud of him."

We should be proud of all of them.

What a great Christmas present, three days early. If there's joy in giving, then these players surely had a blissful sleep when they finally went to bed.

Basketball aids Henson, wife in period of grief

BERNIE BIT • You never know what you're going to get when you sit down with someone and ask questions. Until this interview, Illini coach Lou Henson had been reluctant to discuss his son's death, and I hesitated to ask him about it. But I did, and for some reason, Henson opened his heart to me. Thank you, Lou.

Before each Illinois home game, before every trip, two grieving parents put the real world on hold for a while to visit their only son. They can't hold him or speak with him. But he is still with them. Always.

It is usually morning when Lou and Mary Henson enter the gates of the Mount Hope Cemetery, across from Memorial Stadium in Champaign. There, they pray over the grave of Lou Henson Jr., who was killed Nov. 20 in a single-car accident near Urbana. "We go every day if we can," said Henson, 60. "The cemetery is right across from the stadium. They opened up a beautiful new area and he's there. We like that, and he would like that."

Lou Jr. was 35. Friends of the family say that Lou Jr. was restless for much of his life, not knowing what he wanted to do. But Lou Jr. had found a direction: coaching. He was a first-year head coach at Parkland College, a junior college in Champaign.

"Lou Jr. was a good guy," Illini center Deon Thomas said. "I'd go over to see him. He was somebody you could talk to. He was sincere with you. He was so happy, coaching and working with young people. It's just really sad."

The younger Henson left behind two daughters (ages 12 and 9) and two sweet parents who still struggle to cope with their loss.

"It's hard to explain to anybody, if you haven't gone through it," Henson said. "Mary and I have lost our dads and our moms. But when you lose a son or a daughter, it's completely different. It was devastating. Just devastating. It still is.

"It's the toughest thing we've ever gone through. You just can't express exactly how it is. You try to get through this day, and if you get through this day, then you try to get through the next day."

Basketball is Lou Henson's retreat, the project that occupies his energy and thoughts. Basketball has helped fill Henson's sense of loss. But when the season is over, the void will expand. The pain of Nov. 20 will ache anew.

Lou Jr. died five days before the Illini opened the season against Dayton in a tournament in Alaska. The family buried him on a Monday. On Tuesday, Lou and Mary rejoined the team in Anchorage.

"We had a video tape of the funeral service, and every free moment we would look at that," Henson said. "I don't know how many times we saw it up there. We had two nephews who preached the service and sang. It seemed that every time we see that, there's some relief. We would look at that and celebrate his life."

In his first meeting with his players after the death, Henson repeated a quote from a Martin Luther King Jr. speech: "We either pull together or we will pull apart." It was one of Lou Jr.'s favorite expressions.

"That's become our slogan," Thomas said.

It has been a season of tender mercies.

"Coach never directly talks about what happened," point guard Rennie Clemons said. "But now, when we're leaving after practice, he'll tell us, `Be careful out there.' He never said that before. This is his way of relating back to the accident.

"I know deep down, late at night, he thinks about it. He can't help from doing that. Right now he's got something to occupy his mind — the basketball. Once that ends, he'll have more time to think about it, and it will really hurt him."

If you need a reason to cheer for the Illini, this is it.

Long may they run, so Lou Henson can have an outlet for his emotions.

"Basketball is unbelievable, what it's meant this season," Henson said. "It's not that we don't want to think about Lou, but you can't do that all the time. Basketball does take your mind off of the sadness."

What happens in those quiet, empty moments when Lou and Mary are at home with their memories?

"We've done a lot of reading, and that has helped us," Henson said. "People have sent material to us about dealing with a tragedy. And Lou's two children, our grandchildren, are going to class to learn how to deal with this better.

"We're going to take the grandchildren back to New Mexico, where Lou spent the first part of his life. Because this is good therapy for them. We want them to see the gym he played in. Take them into the homes that we lived in. They'll see where their dad lived. It's going to be good for us, too."

Did anything positive come out of Lou's premature death?

"We can endure anything now," Henson said. "Basketball is very important. Winning has a place, and we probably work at it harder than we did before.

"But it puts everything in the right perspective. It's unfortunate that it took something like this to put it in the right perspective. You can't compare it to anything. Nothing can compare to this."

03.20.1992

Mother Nature helps
Norm light up Tigers

BERNIE BIT • Norm Stewart was always good for a show, but this was my personal favorite. Strange things always seemed to happen when Mizzou entered the NCAA Tournament, and this game may have been the weirdest of all. This opening-round win featured Norm Stewart at his absolute best as a berserk competitor; he just refused to allow his team to lose this one.

GREENSBORO, N.C.

With the arena eerily dark during the first of three blackouts that colored one of the weirdest games in NCAA Tournament history, the bespectacled spokesman from the NCAA offered a detailed scientific explanation.

"Basically, as you can tell," the guy said, with a serious demeanor, "we are having some power problems." No kidding, Mr. Edison.

"We are not losing power," he said. "We are having severe blips of no power. Instantaneous blips."

Right. Those darned instantaneous blips. And that concludes another episode of "Ask Mr. Science."

You just knew this would be difficult for Norm Stewart.

You just knew that something bizarre would have to happen before this tortured man could win again in the NCAA Tournament. His personal streak had lasted 10 years, assuming a cruel life of its own. And now Missouri madness was about to take a surreal turn.

Parapsychology? The strange and powerful forces of the annual Missouri Psychodrama gathered in the North Carolina countryside, rolled ominously into Greensboro, formed into lightning bolts and zapped the power out of a dilapidated arena.

Stewart, who wanted to win this game so desperately that he removed his suit coat and stomped around his sideline like a taller and more overstimulated Rollie Massimino, willed his team over West Virginia.

Glaring and waving like an angry traffic cop, Stewart stalked before his bench. He shrieked at players, browbeat the officials, sweated profusely. He paused only to gulp down hearty swigs of water. It was fascinating. It was frightening. It was Norm.

After one of many horrendous calls went against Mizzou in

the second half, Stewart brought his hands together in front of an alarmed official's face as if to pray for mercy. Other than having an out-of-body experience, Stewart couldn't have coached any harder. He, too, blew a fuse.

Though he downplayed it afterward — "I don't sense that it was anything different," he said — there was no way Stewart would allow Mizzou to lose this game. No more first-round knockouts. No more humiliation. No more questions about why he couldn't win the big one, in the big dance, away from his home turf in the Big Eight.

"I knew he was fired up when he had his jacket off and in the four years I've been here, he's never had his jacket off," said Mizzou's Anthony Peeler, who scored 25 points. "The fire in our eyes came from his and he just kept digging into us and brought it out of us."

Stewart's intensity, so contagious, was strong enough to summon that lightning down from the sky and park it on the roof of this old basketball house. He was an instantaneous blip.

"Coach was like a ghost, whispering to us on the sideline," forward Jamal Coleman said. "He willed us to win. It was like we had six players to their five."

The poor Mountaineers had no chance. Like every Missouri Psychodrama, this was beyond their control. We were all prisoners to it, inside the Greensboro Coliseum.

"That's the strangest game I've ever coached in," West Virginia coach Dale Catlett said. "In 30 years of coaching."

Catlett still doesn't know what hit him. Mizzou needed breathers — and the three lengthy blackouts were made to order — to keep pace with WVU. Missouri had seven players in the rotation. Catlett's plan was to wear down the Tigers; he used 11 players in the first half. But Mizzou used the raw force of those lightning bolts to revamp its own energy supply, surviving despite having two players foul out and three others saddled with four fouls.

Stewart made valuable use of the unorthodox timeouts by motivating his team as it cooled down in the locker room during the dark spells.

When the lights went down the second time, Missouri trailed 38-34 after blowing an eight-point lead. From that point, Mizzou outscored West Virginia 55-40.

The third power shortage, with 1:39 left in the game, was an aggravation. "Is it still Thursday?" Stewart muttered near the locker room before play resumed.

It was still Thursday, and after 10 years and six days and three power blackouts, Norm Stewart had won another game in the NCAA Tournament. All he needed was the lightning. He supplied the thunder.

"It is easy to succeed when the body is young, powerful and loose. But how about when you're ... breaking down physically at the end of a career? What about having to deal with a mind filled with self-doubt? Jackie Joyner-Kersee faced that frustrating set of circumstances."

VARIETY

Wehrli joins Hall with class he showed on the field

BERNIE BIT • I made the presentation to convince the other Hall of Fame voters to support Roger Wehrli, and when the longshot bid came in, it was the happiest I'd ever been as a sportswriter.

CANTON, Ohio

Roger Wehrli made it through his speech without a blip. He did not cry, get choked up or break down. Wehrli was as smooth as ever, gliding through his prepared remarks with the grace and sincerity of a man who never lost his cool as a calm and confident, shut-down cornerback for the old St. Louis Cardinals.

But after thanking a large number of folks who helped shape his life and his career during the path to the Pro Football Hall of Fame, Wehrli walked from the podium and could no longer suppress his swelling emotions.

"I was able to get through the speech and now I'm crying," Wehrli said, after his nine-minute address.

After such a long wait for this special day, Wehrli should have cried a river — the Missouri River, to be exact. After all, he was born and played high school football in King City, Mo. He starred in college football at Mizzou. He was drafted in the first round by the football Cardinals in 1969 and spent his entire 14-year NFL career in St. Louis.

"A true Missourian," said Wehrli's presenter, Cardinals Hall of Famer Larry Wilson.

After earning five All-Pro and seven Pro Bowl honors, Wehrli retired in 1982. Wehrli officially received his overdue acclaim during yesterday's formal induction. He'd been eligible for 20 years.

At times, Wehrli gave up hope that he'd ever make it. At last, he completed an incredible journey that began in King City and ended in the kingdom of pro football. King City has a population of 1,012, but the Pro Football Hall of Fame is even smaller, with only 241 enshrinees.

Wehrli was joined in Canton by around 260 family members and friends. Some important people were missing, however. Roger's father, Russel, died in 1985, and his mother, Margaret, died three years ago. Both parents were teachers and coaches who instilled the values that helped Wehrli reach the pinnacle of his profession.

"If I have one regret, it's that my parents did not live to see this day,"

"At times, Wehrli gave up hope that he'd ever make it. At last, he completed an incredible journey that began in King City and ended in the kingdom of pro football."

Wehrli said. But later he added: "I'm just thankful that so many others could be here. It took a long while to get here, but because of that, my three grandkids were able to be here and see this and share it with me. That means so much."

For months now, Wehrli's family and friends have noted his reserved manner. They fretted that he wouldn't fully enjoy the experience.

Gayle Wehrli, his wife of 38 years, said she'd been pestering him for weeks, asking, 'Aren't you excited?' We've been after him to be a little selfish about this," she said. "We told him, 'It's OK this one time to say, 'It's all about me' instead of putting everyone else first."

In introducing Wehrli, Wilson emphasized those magnanimous

ways.

"In a day when players talk about 'Me,' and say 'Look at me, look at me,' Roger is a 'we' person," Wilson said. "He was a team player. He was unselfish. Not just on the field, but it's always been a part of his daily life. Roger has the highest morals of anyone I've ever met."

Wehrli was generous with his praise. He offered gratitude to his football coach at King City, Richard Flanagan, who made the trip to Canton. He thanked four of his coaches at Ol' Mizzou: the late Clay Cooper, the late Dan Devine and the late Al Onofrio — plus John Kadlec, who is very much alive and was in attendance.

From his NFL days, Wehrli thanked Cardinals owner Bill Bidwill and his Cardinals teammates. He also saluted the fans of the old Big Red. Wehrli was the fourth, and most likely last, St. Louis Cardinal to make it into the Pro Football Hall, following Wilson, Dan Dierdorf and Jackie Smith.

"The fans of St. Louis were wonderful," Wehrli said. "They suffered through the cold and the rain and the heat and the humidity to support the Cardinal football team, and they have remained loyal to us old Cardinals who still make St. Louis our home."

Wehrli started to feel the magnitude of this honor the night before, during the induction dinner, when the new inductees were given their official Hall of Fame jackets.

It was also Gayle's birthday, and the audience of about 3,000 people serenaded her with a warm rendition of "Happy Birthday." Gayle couldn't believe it. "Everything that's happening this weekend, it's as if the planets aligned perfectly," she said.

At the end of the dinner, Wehrli and the other new Hall of Famers gathered on a platform in the middle of the auditorium to wave to the crowd and take in the applause.

Wehrli walked to the edge of the stage, and his three grandchildren rushed to embrace him. He leaned down to hug Drew (age 9), Ellie (10) and Lauren (11). And yes, he cried. And he cried some more after the induction. No quarterback could break Wehrli, but this prestigious honor got to him in the most satisfying way.

"Many of you know me as a man of God," the devout Wehrli said, in closing his speech. "I believe that God has guided each and every move I've made. He put the right people in the right places to bring me here, and I thank Him with all of my heart for taking a little guy from a little town with little dreams and making me fit to wear the title of Hall of Famer."

It was a long time coming, but the man from King City finally entered pro football's kingdom. And it was worth the years, worth the tears.

Ever eat toasted ravioli?
If not, this guide's for you

BERNIE BIT • I love our town for all its charming quirks and somewhat peculiar traditions. When I wrote this good-natured piece, I realized that 20 years after moving here, I finally understood St. Louis.

Greetings to the thousands of visitors who have strolled or staggered into St. Louis for the Final Four. I'm not your official host, but I'd like to welcome everyone and offer a basic primer on our city to help make your stay more enjoyable.

It's great to have you all here. St. Louis is ready . . . or not. It reminds me of something native son Yogi Berra said in 1947 when honored by his St. Louis friends. Yogi looked out at the crowd of visitors and well-wishers and said, "I want to thank you for making this day necessary." Indeed. We have to be here so we'll try to be gracious hosts. It's our pleasure.

We hope you had a nice trip. Our town is known for Charles Lindbergh's "Spirit of St. Louis" flight, but given the lack of nonstop flights in and out of St. Louis these days, your travel experience in getting here was probably more reminiscent of the Lewis & Clark expedition. On your drive to downtown, you may have seen the stretch of Interstate 70 known as "Mark McGwire Highway." Just a warning: in honor of McGwire's recent testimony before Congress, it soon may be shut down, via roadblock. I can't explain why; I'm not going to talk about the past.

First, a special welcome to those dearest to my own heart: my fellow sportswriters who by now are burned out after too many nights on the trail and inside hospitality rooms, chronicling the marvels of March Madness. I would like you to know that our town has a superb literary tradition, with a local honor roll of writers, playwrights and poets that includes Maya Angelou, William Burroughs, Gerald Early, Eugene Field, T.S. Eliot, William Inge, A.E. Hotchner, Tennessee Williams, Sara Teasdale, Marianne Moore, Mona Van Duyn, Howard Nemerov and Jonathan Franzen. And let's not forget Whitey Herzog and his heartland classic, "White Rat: A Life in Baseball" published in 1987.

I trust that you will be inspired by these literary giants and live up to their standards as you pound out a column on deadline in 17 minutes with an editor screaming on the phone moments after Monday night's

NCAA championship game.

OK, here's a breakdown of St. Louis as I try to anticipate some of your questions:

What to eat: There are four basic food groups in St. Louis: (1) Budweiser; (2) toasted ravioli (3) thin-crust pizza; (4) grilled pork steaks. But feel free to experiment; you can substitute Bud Light for Budweiser if you like. If you visit one of our many splendid Italian restaurants, you may order the mostaccioli, pronounced locally as "muskacholey," but keep in mind that it's usually reserved for St. Louis weddings.

About those "St. Louis style" ribs: They don't exist. When I travel and visit restaurants across the United States, I always see "St. Louis style ribs" on the menu. Huh? What? Where? It's an urban legend. So don't ask for them, unless you want to get a puzzled look from an irritated waiter.

What's a Billiken?: That's the nickname, and the mascot, for the St. Louis University sports teams. What it represents is open to interpretation, but recent studies suggest that the Billiken symbolizes hopelessly mediocre college basketball.

The fine arts: There are many acclaimed museums in the region. The Art Museum is in Forest Park, as is the History Museum. There's also the funky and hip City Museum downtown (highly recommended for the kids). But as an alternative, the male basketball fans may want to consider the Sauget Ballet, across the river, a short cab ride from downtown. There you will find a variety of future nuclear physicists and brain surgeons paying their way through institutions of higher learning by providing nightly displays of interpretive dance for enthusiastic customers.

Gambling: You can visit one of our riverboat casinos, or bet the horses at nearby Fairmount Park. Or if you are really in the mood to take a big risk, put off dinner for a few hours and try to find a restaurant that stays open later than 10 p.m.

Forest Park: Site of the 1904 World's Fair, which introduced the ice cream cone to America. The World's Fair also popularized a new culinary item, the hot dog.

The Hill: That's the famous Italian neighborhood, and home of some of the finest Italian restaurants in America. It's a safe, clean and friendly neighborhood, and I can't emphasize that enough. Still, I must mention the most famous crime in Hill history. In 1994, Frank Parrino was shot twice in the head by Joseph Monti, age 87, in daylight on a quiet street. Monti told police that he killed Parrino to settle a 38-year-old grudge. It seems that Parrino and another man had broken Monti's jaw in 1956 after he had asked them to refrain from pinching women customers at the Savoy Club, which Monti managed. So let this be a friendly reminder:

mind your manners on The Hill.

Music: Chuck Berry still rocks. But these days St. Louis is the center of country-grammar style hip-hop word play made famous by Nelly, Chingy, J-Kwon and Cardinals broadcaster Mike Shannon.

Celebrity sightings: We're a little low, unless Cedric the Entertainer, John Goodman or omnipresent broadcaster Joe Buck are hanging out. But those with a fondness for bad 1960s and '70s sitcom TV may want to visit the St. Louis "Walk of Fame" on the Delmar Loop. There in the sidewalks you'll see imbedded plaques honoring St. Louisans Buddy Ebsen ("Beverly Hillbillies"), Agnes Moorehead ("Bewitched"), Redd Foxx ("Sanford and Son") and Robert Guillaume ("Soap" and "Benson"). One glaring oversight is the late Mary Frann, who played Bob Newhart's wife on "Newhart."

How to tell if you are speaking to an authentic St. Louisan: The person will be friendly, polite, courteous, classy, helpful. They'll also ask, "Where did you go to high school?" It's a Lou thing. No need to answer.

One final smile brings comfort to a grieving son

BERNIE BIT • I think about my father every day, and there are times when I can feel him with me, and it will be like that for the rest of my life.

It's great to be back to work, great to be back with you. As some of you know, my father died on Jan. 31, and I wanted to thank all of you who called, sent cards or flowers, or wrote e-mails to offer support. Your tender mercies helped more than you'll know.

We knew he was dying. The doctors told us around Thanksgiving that it was a matter of time, so our family was able to prepare. But how do you really prepare for that shocking moment when your father takes his last breath? I'd left the Super Bowl early to be by his side. I reached the hospital, grabbed his hand, told him I was there, and saw him smile at me. He slipped into a comatose state a few hours later, and died four days later. I am grateful that I was able to be with him in his final days. I slept on a couch in his hospital room, making sure that he would not die alone. And he didn't; at the end he was surrounded by loved ones.

I wanted to be there for him, because I left home in 1985 and hadn't been there for him as his health continued to deteriorate. It wasn't easy, being a thousand miles away as he struggled. I feel as if I let him, and my family, down. But that one smile in the hospital made it all better. I was supposed to be comforting him; instead he comforted me. Once again the father came through for the son.

He taught me how to throw a baseball. He hit grounders and pop flies in the back yard. He went to all of my games. He patted me on the head in the car after I'd allowed a game-winning homer in a showdown for first place. He took me to those glorious Sunday afternoons of Colts football at Memorial Stadium in Baltimore, where we would sit in Section 32 Lower with about 25 other family members who were original Colts season-ticket holders. Those were the best days of our lives.

He knew all the shortcuts to the stadium, tricks that would serve me well for many years. We didn't have much money, but he got the good box seats, third-base side, near Brooks Robinson, for Orioles games. And he would insist that a previous third baseman, George Kell, was better than Brooks — an opinion that I simply could not endorse. So he taught me how to debate sports, too.

He taught me how to tie my shoes, how to put on a tie. He boosted my budding love for journalism by bringing me all of the newspapers on his way home from work. He'd gently tell me to calm down when I hollered at the TV set over an official's call, or a bad play. He gave his crying boy a hug after the Colts lost Super Bowl III, and then again when the Orioles were upset by the Mets. (Oh, how we despised the New York teams.) He ordered me not to throw baseballs against the side of the house — I kept breaking shingles — but never really minding when I did. He'd read my little hand-written stories that I'd produce when we returned home from watching a game. He was calm and in control when I wrecked my first car. He took me to the bank to open my first account.

He was there, always.

And now what? I can't replace him. But he's definitely with me. My father didn't have an easy life. He had epilepsy and suffered from frequent seizures. I'll never forget being at the hospital as a small boy, watching a Catholic priest give my father the last rites. That was in the mid-1960s. But my father rallied, battled back. He always did. We were fortunate to have him for as long as we did. But health complications limited his employment opportunities and career advancement. He couldn't travel much. He was passed over for promotions. He wasn't able to pursue all of his dreams. Limitations were imposed on him.

But he never complained. He was never bitter. He never asked, "Why me?" He just went to work at the same desk in the same government office for 40 years, earned a modest salary, did a good job, stayed married to the same woman for 46 years, raised three children, gave us a good life.

In his final couple of years, he lost the ability to walk, talk, and eat solid food. How cruel is that — to be unable to enjoy life's basic necessities and pleasures? And yet he smiled through it all. He wanted to keep going. He never cursed his fate. It was remarkable.

And I've been thinking about that a lot. I compare it to how upset I get over trivial, meaningless matters. I compare his strength to my weakness. I wish I had his quiet toughness. His dignity. His grace. His boundless optimism.

Bernie Miklasz Sr. was never the type to sit down and give advice. He led by example. He still is, even in death. I am writing this column on my birthday. Naturally, I am thinking about him a lot. How he led his life, the way he successfully endured so much adversity, and his valiant struggle to live, even as it appeared that he had little reason to want to persevere. He has inspired me to try and become a better man. It's really the best tribute I can offer him.

09.14.2001

To grieving nation, sports are much more than merely games

BERNIE BIT • My first inclination after the Sept. 11 terrorist attacks was to forget about sports, including the writing of sports columns, for a while. But through the years, I've learned that sports can unite us, and therefore have value.

Late Thursday morning, NFL Commissioner Paul Tagliabue decided to call off the games scheduled for this weekend. The NCAA Division I-A schools that hadn't already called off their games followed the NFL's lead and abandoned plans to play. And late Thursday afternoon, Commissioner Bud Selig announced that Major League Baseball put off its plans to resume its schedule until Monday.

Those who oversee sports determined that it was too soon to head back into the stadiums and the ballparks for fun and recreation, even if the games would provide a positive therapeutic effect. In the NFL, especially, passionate feelings took over. Coaches, players and owners just didn't believe it was appropriate to proceed as if Tuesday morning hadn't happened. They could not ignore the wound to our national psyche. And Tagliabue provided excellent leadership, proving that he's in touch with the prevailing sentiment around the league and across the nation. The other sports quickly fell into line with Tagliabue's judgment.

It was too much to ask the New York Giants to host a Sunday game in a stadium situated only 12 miles from the disaster site in Manhattan. It was too much to ask the Washington Redskins to play a home game in a stadium that's a short, suburban drive from the Pentagon. The Giants' practice-field bubble has been designated as a temporary morgue for victims. The parking lot at Giants Stadium is being utilized as a command post for rescue efforts.

"Our work is very important to all of us, but I just don't think that it's right to play a game right now," Rams general manager Charley Armey said. "Not when we're watching real American heroes digging through all of the rubble trying to save lives."

There is room in our democracy for disagreement on all issues, including the role of sports in our culture during tragic times. Many good Americans who love sports are searching inward, trying to balance a blend of powerful, conflicting feelings.

"The pain that's here now will be there a week from now, a year from now, a generation from now. If sports aren't important, then play should be suspended indefinitely. But sports can help unite, and heal, the nation."

I was touched by comments made by Emmitt Smith, the splendid running back for the Dallas Cowboys. He has been watching TV all week, seeing the suffering in New York and in Washington, and he's frustrated by his inability to make a difference.

"The best way, other than to give blood or money, is probably to go out and play so people can get a break from what they are looking at and maybe watch this," Smith told reporters in Dallas. "I was thinking that maybe if the game was played, instead of being pounded all day every day with all this agony and sadness, it might be a good outlet."

That sums up why I would have supported Tagliabue if he had decided to move ahead with this week's NFL schedule. But there is no absolute right or wrong here. A lot of pure hearts are beating faster as we struggle to cope with every aspect of this national crisis.

And certainly we can all get by without a weekend of football and baseball. That was never the point, anyway. Those of us who advocated the resumption of games did so out of a sincere belief that sports are a symbol of America's strength and spirit. And that we could use sports as a way to send a message around the globe that we will not be forced into seclusion by evil deeds.

This is complicated, to say the least. Those of you who believe that it was inappropriate and insensitive to even consider playing games so soon after the terrorist attack, I would never say you're wrong. But I ask: Where do we draw the boundaries? Is it inappropriate to head to the movie theaters this weekend? Or to eat at your favorite restaurant? What about that scheduled tee time for Saturday morning? Or a weekend getaway to the lake? Should all entertainment-recreational activities be suspended?

If we're going to have a period of mourning this weekend, then let's do it right. Let's go all the way with it, instead of cherry-picking to accommodate our specific set of sensibilities.

And I just wonder what will be different a week from now.

It is likely that victims will still be missing.

Heroic rescue workers will likely be searching for bodies.

It is likely that families will still be in the process of burying loved ones.

The once-magnificent towers in New York will still be down.

The Pentagon will still be torn apart.

We will still be grieving. We will still be shaken. The hole in our collective soul will still be there.

And the sports stadiums — an easy and inviting target for terrorists — will still be sitting there, as vulnerable as ever.

Will New York's football and baseball teams, and Washington's NFL team, feel significantly more comfortable playing a game next weekend?

Calling off the games makes us feel good, because it seemed like the right thing to do.

But someone please explain why cheering and dancing in a stadium is considered out of line this weekend, only to be deemed as acceptable behavior next weekend.

I just didn't realize that we can put a time clock on mourning.

The pain that's here now will be there a week from now, a year from now, a generation from now.

If sports aren't important, then play should be suspended indefinitely.

But sports can help unite, and heal, the nation. That's why President George W. Bush reportedly encouraged the sports leagues to return to action.

And for that reason alone, sports can provide an immediate and valuable contribution to our anguished culture. The sooner the better.

Jordan battles illness, adds to legend in win

BERNIE BIT • I felt privileged to watch Michael Jordan in his prime, refusing to succumb. This was a true Legend of Jordan moment. He called me "Big Fella" once during a press conference. We were tight. (Not really.)

SALT LAKE CITY

Michael Jordan was ailing. Blame it on the flu. Or food poisoning. Maybe he was just allergic to losing, infected by his teammates' fears, or just plain sick of Utah.

Jordan was nauseated before Game 5. Puffy-faced. Sweating profusely. In need of a cool washcloth, a warm bed. Jordan had the vacant look of a zombie. His bloodshot eyes were slits. He moved slowly in the pregame warm-ups as if unsure of his balance. "He was listless, he couldn't sit up; I've never seen him like that," Chicago Bulls center Luc Longley said. "I didn't think he could play."

Jordan spent all day in misery, sleeping or rushing to the bathroom. The Bulls should have hooked him up to an IV unit. Instead, Jordan became intravenous energy for the Bulls. He was their life-support system.

Jordan can't call in sick, not when his teammates are overcome by fear, overwhelmed by the cacophony inside the Delta Center, and rattled by the Jazz. Legends don't take the day off or call for the nurse. Legends keep producing new fables, new episodes of wonder.

Facing the franchise's most important game of the decade, the Bulls needed Jordan to rescue them again. And last night, before the nation, Jordan gave what might have been the defining performance of his brilliant career.

Jordan scored 38 points — including the winning 3-pointer — grabbed seven rebounds, made three steals and had five assists to personally capture a 90-88 victory for the Bulls in Game 5 of the best-of-seven NBA finals.

This was one from Jordan's heart. A classic. This was Muhammad Ali in Manila. This was Kirk Gibson limping around the bases after the winning homer in Game 1 of the 1988 World Series. This was Willis Reed dragging a bad leg out to the court for Game 7 to inspire the New York Knicks. This was Bob Gibson pitching on a broken leg.

One for the ages. It left us speechless, Jordan speechless. Dehydrated after the game, Jordan couldn't come to the interview room. And that was OK. "His body language said it all," Longley said.

This was why we still care about sports, why these games are worth all of the money, frustration and heartache. Jordan reminded us.

"I've played many seasons with Michael, and I've never seen him as sick to the point where I didn't even think he could put the uniform on," teammate Scottie Pippen said. "And somehow he just showed how big a professional he is by gutting this game out and staying in there. He felt like he was going to pass out. But he gave us the performance we needed. There's nothing else to say. He's the greatest."

In the fourth quarter, with the Bulls down by as many as eight points, Jordan scored 15 points. He found energy when most people would have collapsed. In the key sequence, MJ hit the first of two foul shots to tie the game at 85-85. Jordan missed the second free throw, but scuffled for the rebound.

A couple of passes later, the ball was in Jordan's hands. Money time. He was instant medicine, baby. Chicken soup for Bulls fans. Jordan dropped the 3-pointer for an 88-85 Chicago lead, making Jazz fans weak in the knees.

During breaks the Bulls fanned Jordan with cool towels, applied ice packs to the back of his neck, poured fluids down his throat, splashed him with ice water. Jordan — heaving, sweating, head down — kept rising from his seat. He kept finding the generator, the will to go on.

Jordan silenced Utah's motormouth, Bryon Russell, who made the foolish mistake of calling Jordan "Michelle."

Uh-oh. Jordan has napalmed trash-talking opponents throughout his career, leaving burn marks all over the NBA. Russell was scorched in Game 5.

And the kid — the poor knucklehead — still doesn't get it. After the game, Russell said, "No, I don't think Jordan was sick. You media guys think he was sick. You guys keep saying he was sick, but he sure didn't look sick."

Russell doesn't understand that Jordan thrives on challenges and adversity. And MJ came up empty at the end of Game 4, handing a gift victory to the Jazz.

We sensed what would happen next. It's like the end of Jordan's latest Nike commercial, when he says: "I've failed over and over again in my life. And that is why I succeed."

On a very special night, we saw Jordan succeed again. But we witnessed something more profound: the greatest athlete of his generation, taking his legend higher.

Jordan, sick and exhausted, was suspended in a dream state. Instead of falling down, he elevated his reputation to dazzling new heights. Jordan hangs above the NBA. He floats among the stars now.

Bronze medal a badge of honor for JJK

BERNIE BIT • I've never covered a more tenacious athlete than JJK. Past her athletic prime, and debilitated by injury, this last Olympic medal was the result of her greatest attribute: pure will.

ATLANTA

The bronze medal around Jackie Joyner-Kersee's collar shined like gold, and was just as valuable. This wasn't any medal; this was mettle. A badge of honor. So much went into this bronze.

Pain. Grit. Age. Fears. Sweat.

"That medal is made of heart," said Bobby Kersee, Jackie's husband/coach. "That's a medal of courage."

On this special night, third place in the long jump was just as worthy as finishing first. And Jackie Joyner-Kersee, who has set the right example in so many ways, offered another view of her extraordinary character.

It is easy to succeed when the body is young, powerful and loose. It is easy to win when an athlete is in peak form, and everything feels right and the confidence is soaring.

But how about when you're 34 and breaking down physically at the end of a career? What about having to deal with a mind filled with self-doubt? How about competing with a balky, wrapped-up right hamstring that felt like an anchor, holding you back, keeping you earthbound?

Jackie Joyner-Kersee faced that frustrating set of circumstances, and she won. No, not the gold medal. But she still won, anyway. She held off the erosion of time. She persevered through the increased wear and tear. She overcame the biting hamstring. She conquered any thoughts of surrendering to the pain. She gritted her teeth and went after her final goal.

"She had to scrape her body up to the medal podium," Bobby Kersee said. "She's never worked harder for anything."

In a hallway, Jackie was asked if winning this bronze was more satisfying than taking home previous gold medals. "Absolutely," she said. "Absolutely."

And this is how Jackie asked to be remembered:

"That I always gave 100 percent, all the time," she said. "Always trying to find a way to win. Even when I came up short, I never gave up."

And this will be her legacy. Since her first Olympics (1984), we have been dazzled by Joyner-Kersee's athleticism. Last night, we were left to celebrate her resolve, her absolute willpower, her essence.

JJK had six jumps.

The first five were weak.

The first five were not Jackie. She flopped into sixth place. Joyner-Kersee had little speed on the runway, no thrust on takeoff. Joyner-Kersee appeared finished. Done. Burned out. Doomed by the hamstring that yanked her straight out of the heptathlon competition, prompting a sympathetic phone call from President Clinton.

Everyone was feeling sorry for the greatest woman athlete to ever grace the Olympics. This was not the way JJK wanted to go out. She's tough.

And then came her sixth jump.

Last chance, after four Olympics and five medals (three of them gold).

Would there be a sixth Olympic medal?

Deep breath . . . everyone in Olympic stadium . . . and East St. Louis . . . and St. Louis . . . her friends in Los Angeles . . . her multitude of fans throughout the world . . . deep breath . . . crossed fingers . . . away we go.

More than 80,000 fans cheered her on with all the volume they could pump from their lungs.

Jackie gathered her thoughts and talked to herself.

"I just knew I had to give it my best shot," she said. "It was really difficult at that point. The hamstring hurt and I was trying not to punish myself mentally. I wanted to be positive, and not think about the pain.

"This was the last one. So I said, `Don't give up. Just don't give up. You can still do it.' I wanted to run as hard as I could, and really take off. If the muscle goes, it goes. It would hurt, but I would have no regrets."

She was up in the air now, and her feet touched down in bronze. And for the cynics and sports-haters who don't understand why intelligent people get caught up in these little dramas — for those who come to the Olympics and sneer at the concept of the "human spirit" — well, this jump was for you fools, too.

Joyner-Kersee seemed disappointed by her final jump; was it good enough to scoot up into third place? The crowd let her know. Yes! They roared in sustained applause. Joyner-Kersee turned and waved. For the first time all week, she smiled.

"I think she uplifted the people of the world," Bobby Kersee said. "I don't think she realized how many people cared about her, and how happy she made them. She didn't get to hear the national anthem, but they still raised that American flag. She could see what she did for her country."

It was an hour after the jump now, and Bobby Kersee sat off to the side in the interview room, as Jackie answered questions about snatching the bronze with the last-gasp leap.

A doctor came over, and handed him some pain medication for Jackie. And she needed it. Bobby removed his glasses and rubbed his eyes. He was drained, too. It had been an exhausting, worrisome week for the Joyner-Kersee family and entourage. But one jump made it all right.

One final jump that confirmed everything we knew about Jackie Joyner-Kersee: that she's a champion. But last night, we also learned something new. That a bronze medal can be worth more than a gold.

It's a vault of gold for U.S. gymnasts

BERNIE BIT • I learned something valuable here; toughness has nothing to do with size or musculature. I never thought anything could move me to turn all mushy over gymnastics, until this memorable display of grit at the Atlanta Olympics.

ATLANTA

She knew something was wrong when she crash-landed the first time.

Kerri Strug heard a pop, and now her left ankle was burning in pain, screaming "NO" to her. Her coach, Bela Karolyi, was shouting "YES," telling her to go. Her teammates looked at her with pleading eyes.

"I was so scared," Strug said. Her littlest teammate, Dominique Moceanu, had just missed on two vaults. Strug slipped on her own first try. The Russians were still a threat to snatch the gold, or so everyone thought. Strug was the last to compete in the rotation, and the U.S. women couldn't afford a second consecutive poor score on the vault apparatus.

The scoreboard — flashing all those blinking numbers — offered no guarantees. So Kerri Strug knew what she had to do. She had to save the gymnastics gold medal for the U.S. women. The moment would not wait for her to heal. The moment would not make an exception for her little-girl fears. Strug had to make an adult choice.

"All the hard work and effort we had put in for all those years," Strug said. "It felt like everything was slipping away. I felt I had to do it. I owed it to everyone."

She eyed the vault down at the end of the runway. The mission: On a damaged ankle, Strug had to go for the gold. Sprint as fast as possible, catapult her body into the air and over the vault, then tinker with the forces of gravity for a solid landing.

One deep breath. Then a second.

Big eyes staring straight ahead.

Dangling her foot. Rolling it around. Now it felt numb. The buzz through the Georgia Dome indicated fear and confusion. Strug had to block out everything. She set her feet on the mat. Think. Concentrate. Lock in.

Finally it was time to go. The world would be watching the biggest and most poignant moment of an 18-year-old's life. She was no longer a cute little ornament, a delicate doll pulled from the box to delight adults once every four years in the Olympics. No, Kerri Strug was about to become a good, old-fashioned American hero. She was about to plant her tiny feet firmly into history.

"I kind of said a little prayer," Strug said. "Please God, help me out here. I've got to do this one more time. I've done it thousands and thousands of times. I need it again."

She was gone now, big eyes alarmed and wide open. Carrying her own dreams, her teammates' goals and the hopes of every gymnastics fan in the nation. So much might in such a small package. Less than 100 pounds, but tougher than any 260-pound football player that you can think of.

She said her prayer. Kerri Strug was off and running, up and over — a wounded butterfly, somehow continuing in majestic flight. She landed. The left ankle all but came unhinged, with two outside ligaments tearing apart. Somehow, she managed to stand for an instant, to preserve the balanced pose and ring up the judges' points.

They gave Kerri Strug a good score — 9.712 — and the team gold belonged to the USA. Strug hopped in pain, her eyes dampened by tears. She fell down. A stretcher was called. As they carried Strug out, the U.S. realized that gold had been clinched. The Russians finished second. The American girls celebrated, with the Georgia Dome hugging them with theater-in-the-round cheers.

Strug, crying and oblivious, had given up her immediate health and a spot in Thursday's all-around individual finals. An unbelievable scene of all that is right and wrong with gymnastics. So much glory, so many medals and all those broken bodies piled up outside the gymnasium door.

In a touching, warm-and-fuzzy sequence, Karolyi carried Strug in his arms and back to the mat, setting her softly on the podium to be with her six teammates and savor the gold-medal ceremony. No one deserved it more than Strug, who begged Bela not to let doctors take her to the hospital until she had had a chance to slip on the big gold necklace with her friends. Bela scooped her up, and we had the No. 1 moment of the 1996 Olympics. This teenage flower stood in the center of the Georgia Dome and cried during the National Anthem. Nothing in the Games to come can exceed this tear-jerker.

"What she gave us was a striking moment of courage, willpower, toughness and sacrifice," Karolyi said. "I'm very proud of her. She could have very easily said no to the second vault. I told her, `We need this vault.' She told me she couldn't feel anything in her leg. But I told her, `One more time. Shake it off, do your best.' She responded like a little angel. This was an act of courage that made history for the U.S. The first gold medal for the women."

Did Karolyi act irresponsibly for pushing Strug?

"It's difficult for people on the outside to understand," gymnast Dominique Dawes said. "We train for 10 years or more to achieve something like this. The dream is right in front of you, and it comes down to enduring pain for a 10-second vault. If you come to that choice, you do it."

Besides, the decision was Strug's. She was going to conquer that vault, no matter what the coaches told her. "I'm 18 years old," Strug said. "I can make my own choices. Everyone had put so much into this, and this was a lifelong dream of mine. I couldn't give up. Definitely, yes, I wanted to do it. I've been through so much pain before, one last vault, I can deal with it."

Three hours after her injury and a trip to the hospital, she returned to the dome on crutches to sit for an interview.

Finally, someone asked Kerri Strug if she felt like a hero. She laughed in a voice that seemed much younger than her 18 years. This was comforting, to hear that darling laugh.

"I hope everyone realizes that it took a lot of guts to go out and do my second vault," Strug said. "Because it really hurt."

Her father, Burt, watched from a corner. Kerri's mom, Melanie, clutched her daughter's bouquet of victory flowers. I asked Burt how he felt, watching this incredible drama unfold around his flesh and blood.

"It was a dream and it was a nightmare," he said. "Both extremes. But we're proud of her. She's tougher than any of us."

Burt Strug had a notepad in his hands. It had a list of interview requests. All the morning network shows want Kerri to come on. Everyone is calling. She is still Burt and Melanie's daughter, yes. They don't realize it yet, but Kerri Strug belongs to America now.

In home of the shrine, a mother finally smiles

BERNIE BIT • Dan Dierdorf is one of my favorite people, and I can't imagine what it would feel like to grow up in Canton, Ohio and later return there to be inducted into the Pro Football Hall of Fame. The sentiment must be overwhelming.

For the third year in a row, Evelyn Dierdorf sat by the phone in her home in Canton, Ohio. Two of her friends kept her company. She was nervous. It was the Saturday before the Super Bowl. Election day again.

Evelyn soon would learn if her son, Dan Dierdorf, had been voted into the Pro Football Hall of Fame. The shrine stands a mile from the Dierdorf home in Canton. Dan was born in the house where Evelyn, a widow, still lives. "If it wasn't for a few trees and some hills, I could probably see the football stadium next to the Hall of Fame," she said. "So close."

And so far. For the past two years Dan Dierdorf had reached the final ballot in the Hall of Fame selection. Both times, those Hall of Fame doors virtually slammed in his face. Dierdorf, the imposing tackle for the St. Louis Cardinals, was denied on the final vote.

Now that he was on the brink again, Dan was more concerned with his mother's feelings than his own. For Evelyn Dierdorf, the waiting was the hardest part: a cruel experience for a woman of 77 to endure.

"This has been a difficult process for all of us, but especially my mother," Dan said. "It just takes a lot out of you. It broke me up to have to call her the last couple of years to comfort her when I didn't make it."

Perhaps this would be — finally — a day of celebration. Or would it be a day of more heartache?

A few minutes after 2 p.m., the phone rang. On the line was Don Dasco, Dan's lifelong friend. "He made it," Dasco told Evelyn. "Dan was voted into the Hall of Fame."

The phone may still be ringing.

"Every time I hang up, someone else calls with their congratulations," Evelyn Dierdorf said. "It's been a wonderful, wonderful, day. A dream come true. I'm so proud of him. He's been such a wonderful son."

Evelyn Dierdorf excused herself. She wanted to stop crying.

"This has been tough, Dan not getting in," she said. "I felt bad for him. But in a way, maybe I'm happier today. When you want something really bad, and you have to wait for it a long time, it's extra special when you

"Dierdorf is a national celebrity ... in ABC's Monday Night Football booth. He was an All-Pro with the St. Louis Cardinals. But in Canton, Dierdorf is just a friend, the big guy."

get it."

Dierdorf is a national celebrity because of his spot in ABC's Monday Night Football booth. He was a football star at the University of Michigan, an All-Pro with the Cardinals.

But in Canton, Dan Dierdorf is just a friend, the big guy. Evelyn and John's youngest of three sons, Dan was born in the house on 36th Street on June 29, 1949. He was baptized at Trinity United Church of Christ and was a large, awkward but promising lineman and wrestler at Glenwood High. He was the best buddy that Dasco, Tom Anthony or John Noyes could ever have.

Dierdorf thinks so much of their friendship that every March he takes his three boyhood pals to Florida for a week of golf. Dierdorf pays for everything.

"I've known him from the first grade, and went with him all the way through high school," Dasco said. "And Dan is no different than he was then. He's a blue-collar, funny, down-to-earth, caring man. He has a successful career and his cup is overflowing, but he's the same person.

That's why everyone likes him here so much. There are a lot of tears flowing today in Canton."

Evelyn Dierdorf said that perhaps as many as 500 friends and family from Canton will attend Dan's induction in July. But one person won't be there: Dierdorf's father, who worked most of his life for the Hoover Vacuum Co. in Canton, died after a heart attack 14 years ago.

"His father was Dan's idol," Dasco said. "When Dan comes back to Canton, the first thing he does is go visit the cemetery. If Dan could have one wish in his life I'm sure it would be to have his dad there with him on the day he goes into the Hall of Fame."

Said Evelyn Dierdorf: "When Dan talks about his father as he gives his speech at the Hall of Fame, I hope he can get through that part. It will be very emotional for him."

Dan was with his father the first time he saw the Hall of Fame's site.

"I was there with my dad for the ground-breaking ceremonies," Dierdorf said. "We watched the building being built. I went to every enshrinement ceremony until I went away to college. It's impossible for me to comprehend that it could mean more to somebody than it does to me. It's the thrill of my life."

Town without sports keeps head in the game

BERNIE BIT • I remember this dark, bizarre period in my career as a sports columnist. I'd wake up in the morning and have no idea what I'd write about. Somehow, I managed to fill five columns a week, and I still don't know how I did it.

This must be the strangest, weirdest phase in the history of professional sports in St. Louis. People, we have no major-league sports.

We have maybe the best — certainly the newest — sports facilities in the nation. But no sports.

We have a gorgeous $135 million arena. And it is a doll house. Beautiful to look at, but nothing real inside. Still, more than 35,000 fans filed through the Kiel over the weekend, just to gawk.

We have the mad genius of hockey coaches, Mike Keenan, but he isn't coaching. We have nothing for the man to do. He just keeps wandering around in fancy double-breasted suits, receiving standing ovations, taking bows.

We have the continent's top hockey arena. We have no hockey.

We have Keenan. We have no games for Keenan.

Instead, we have the Kiel Center Partners throwing exclusive black-tie parties to heap praise on themselves. If Jud Perkins pats himself on the back one more time, I'm gonna kiel over.

Gary Bettman, the diminutive commissioner with the equally small mind, won't allow the National Hockey League season to begin. Memo to Bettman, the smug New York lawyer: When you market your expensive product all summer, when you accept season-ticket money from fans on a budget, when thousands of loyal puckheads have spent the last several months scrimping and saving and manipulating the family finances on good faith to purchase the NHL's overpriced seats, you have a moral obligation to play the games. Have some integrity. Stop the union-busting and play hockey.

Moving right along . . .

We have a new $260 million football stadium that's about 50 percent completed. But unless the construction workers play a game of touch football, there won't be any action there any time soon.

FANS Inc. is flying to Los Angeles to romance the Rams. During his distinguished political career, Sen. Tom Eagleton never lost an election.

"We're looking forward to the 1995 baseball season, but there might not be a '95 season. We're so starved for baseball that 50,000 showed up at Busch Stadium to run the bases and tour the press box."

Now, as the leader of FANS, Eagleton needs two votes: Georgia Frontiere's and John Shaw's. It'll cost about $70 million to buy this election. Good luck, Senator. Here's an idea: offer the Rams some of Dick Gephardt's PAC money and skip the permanent seat licenses.

We'll have two football stadiums (Busch and the dome). We have no football. And yet, I keep writing columns on the Rams. I am walking the streets wearing a Rams cap, babbling to strangers in sports bars. I am having visions of Jerome Bettis. At night, I play Strat-O-Matic baseball. It has come to this.

Moving right along . . .

We have Mark Lamping. He's the new Cardinals president, and he's so full of crazed, gung-ho exuberance that he's interviewed something like 11,328 people for the team's vacancy at general manager. And on the weekends, Lamping is debating soccer refs and getting tossed from his kid's games. Yes, he's getting red cards at peewee soccer matches.

Lamping already has been ejected more times than Joe Torre. A wild man, this Lamping. The Cardinals need him. We need him. By all indications, he's going to reinvent the Cardinals, give these zombies a personality.

We're looking forward to the 1995 baseball season, but there might not be a '95 season. We have Lamping. We have no baseball. We don't even have Ken Burns to nit-pick anymore. (Ken: Lou Brock. Look into it.) We're so starved for baseball that 50,000 showed up at Busch Stadium (for an open house) to run the bases and tour the press box.

I get calls now. From an editor in Dallas. From a columnist in New York. From radio call-in hosts in Detroit, Atlanta and Denver. They want to know: What's it like being a sports columnist with no major-league sports to write about? Hah, hah. What are the fans doing?

Well, I tell them, we're walking around, thousands strong, filling up empty arenas and stadiums to watch nothing. We're getting excited about women's golf. We're starting fan clubs for an NFL team that plays in LA. We're misty-eyed with joy when our state university loses to Colorado by 15 points in college football.

And the thing is, we're happy. We're smiling. For a town without sports, this is one incredible sports town.

12.26.1993

The birth of Bernie Bits

BERNIE BIT • It was never planned this way, but the Bits became my signature column, and to this day I feel guilty when I take a week off from writing them. I just wish I had more newspaper space every Saturday to include all of the Bits that I've accumulated during the week.

This Bernie Bits thing is out of control. I've created a monster. This concept, initially a weak take-off on colleague Jerry Berger's columns, began as an occasional notes column reserved for those slow news days.

In a bind, I figured I'd fill the space by dropping in a few names, making some quick comments, zapping out a few zingers, plugging a few sports-related charity events.

No big deal.

But the column, once hatched, sprouted and demanded a life of its own. Kind of like the giant plant in "Little Shop Of Horrors."

Actually, the readers demanded the Bits. I'd be out, meet some sports fans. We'd talk about the latest sports news. And then someone would say, "I like that Bernie Bits column. You ought to write more of them."

OK. I added a fifth column per week (too many). A special Bits-only day. Saturday.

I'd get calls, the voice belonging to a volunteer spy: "Yo, I got a Bernie Bit for you." (And the thing is, I hadn't asked for any.)

Then the letters.

"More Bits?"

"We're having a softball tournament to raise money for homeless gerbils. Can you run a Bit on it?"

"I wish you'd forget the other stuff and just write those Bernie Bits every day."

Not all readers felt this way, of course. A terse gentleman rang me up on a call-in program at KMOX, informed me that he objected to my "gossip" column, called me Rona Barrett and said he'd canceled his subscription to the newspaper.

Sorry. This ain't everyone's cup of coffee.

Last summer, I took a sabbatical from the Bits. A month, or so. I was burned-out on Bits.

Big mistake.

I'd be at Busch Stadium: "Hey, why don't you do Bits anymore?"

I'd be dining at a restaurant. Waiter: "Any chance Bits will return?"

A colleague: "Don't let the Bits die."

Bits. Bits. Bits.

My wife critiques them. She tells me that the Bits are a reflection of my mood. She's right. More specifically, they are a reflection of my mood swings.

Only in Bits do you see a merciless cheap shot against Norm Stewart in one paragraph, followed by an appeal to attend a fundraiser for the Juvenile Diabetes Foundation in the next.

People love to see their name in Bits and angle for a mention. . . . then again, some hate to see their name in Bits. I've learned that one biting sentence in Bits can land me in more hot water than two weeks of traditional columns.

It's an erratic column. A berserk column. A confusing journey into the center of my mind.

I'm all over the map. But it's a popular column, apparently.

And perhaps it accomplishes some good on occasion.

Our Arena may be for the birds, but the tradition soars

BERNIE BIT • It's sad that most of the old sporting arenas and stadiums are gone; the modern comforts of antiseptic new sports venues don't come close to matching the character and the history that's been lost.

It's about 48 hours before Indiana and Louisville will open the NCAA Midwest Regional at The Arena, and Fred Corsi is wondering how he's going to get rid of the birds.

They're back, mocking him, taking off on daring flight patterns from a perch high above The Arena floor. This is a scene from Corsi's personal Hitchcock movie. The Birds torture him. Like Tippi Hedren, he must terminate the beasts. Just imagine these evil swallows dive-bombing Bob Knight's huddle during a timeout. Oh, the horror.

Corsi, The Arena's director of operations, is a brave hunter. He clears the birds out, others sneak back, slipping through gaps in the roof. The birds hover, menacing hockey teams, pro wrestlers, college basketball players, fans.

Corsi always makes them disappear.

"We ask them to leave," he said. "And they leave."

Right. After a little nudge. Arena spies tell us that Corsi sets a trap of birdseed and sends in the two Arena cats, Damian and Scorch. If the veteran mousers don't shut down the aviary, Fred calls for the big ammo. He's the only building manager in America who keeps a BB gun next to the Zamboni machine.

Corsi is the best. No operations man does more with less than Corsi, who makes more Arena saves than the Blues' Curtis Joseph. Corsi has the plant in terrific shape for the Midwest Regional.

Visitors to St. Louis: Welcome to our Arena.

The prehistoric barn is a weird place, an antique fun house occupied by two fat cats, friendly mice, birds, mutant ninja crawling things and other members of the wild Animal Kingdom — including Basil McRae.

Do not be alarmed. You are fortunate. There is no NCAA regional like this one. Let the others — those fans in the Seattle Kingdome, the New Jersey Meadowlands and the Charlotte Coliseum — eat meals off immaculate floors.

The Arena has character — and a minor rodent problem. But it was raised for real sports fans, not those imported-bottled-water-sipping yuppies who don't fancy a sports arena unless it's equipped with a private suite and a Jacuzzi.

No, this is a place where cigar smoke comes to die.

It's our eyesore, and we love it.

This deformity on Oakland Avenue is 64 years old, terminally ill, beyond all hope and redemption. It has been scoured, scrubbed, buffed, waxed and treated with miracle chemicals. It has had more facial surgery than Michael Jackson. The ancient roof falls apart worse than the Blues at playoff time. A driving rainstorm turns The Arena basement into a tributary of the Mississippi. The Orkin man lives here. Elvis may live here.

Nothing can beautify this Arena. Nothing can save it. A couple of years from now, The Arena will be dynamited into smithereens. So, unless the Blues qualify for the Stanley Cup finals, this prestigious Midwest Regional will be the last call for a nationally prominent sports event.

So wink at this homely girl, would you?

When it's filled to standing-room-only, The Arena has a combustible atmosphere. The noise threatens to lift the building off its moorings. Your ears will ring.

"It's an exciting place to watch an event because all the sight lines are fantastic," Corsi said. "When it's wild inside, you can feel it in your bones. The fans are right on top of the action. You feel like you can reach down and touch these players. It's something you're never going to have in a new building because you can't design them like that any more.

"On the flip side, the water lines are 63 years old. The sewer lines are bad and deteriorating. Every time it rains — heavy rains with wind — the west side of the building floods. Every time there's much wind, the ceiling tiles blow off and we get new leaks. It's so antiquated in many ways. When you got to maintain it, sometimes you hate this place, but when you have an event here and open up the doors and see the crowds, it just gives you a thrill to be here."

The hardwood court, pounded by basketballs for 35 years, is ready. It's the same oak that UCLA's Bill Walton romped on while scoring a record 44 points in the 1973 NCAA championship game.

The relic scoreboard, 25 years old, is attached to the roof by aircraft cables. The board went haywire late last month, and Corsi's staff spent three weeks finding and fixing the kinks, eliminating the ghost in the machine. Understand that this is like stringing lights on the Christmas Tree from Hell.

"There are 65 individual light banks that have to be checked out when everything goes wrong," he said. "We had a truck pull in here and the truck vibrations did a lot of damage to that board. It vibrated the light

"The Arena was raised for real sports fans, not imported-bottle-water-sipping yuppies. This is a place where cigar smoke comes to die. It's our eyesore, and we love it."

bulbs, loosened them up and shorted them out. We had to take it apart, piece by piece."

When you're seated for Thursday night's games, look skyward. You may be wondering: What are those dirty sheets doing in the rafters? Answer: They're noise baffles. The crew can't wash them because they're wired to the roof, rotting, older than the shroud of Turin. (Really; you can see images in the cloth. One has the face of Marvin Barnes. Scary.)

The Arena represents a dying breed. Here, a new arena is under construction near Union Station. Boston and Chicago are erecting new palaces. The old arenas are an endangered species. We're going upscale and sterile. Luxury will be gained. Tradition will be lost.

Creatures of comfort may be disoriented, but I hope Arena visitors can enjoy this archaic monstrosity, with all its quirks and eccentricities. Where else will a cat crawl onto your lap while you watch basketball, looking to share your popcorn? That's Damian. Biggest mooch in town.

"Hopefully, Damian won't scratch Bob Knight," Corsi said.

Hey, the cat doesn't have that many lives.

Winning championship would be special for Stallings and son

BERNIE BIT • I played a strange role in Alabama football history. I wrote a column criticizing the Arizona Cardinals for failing to extend Gene Stallings' contract. The column included some negative comments from a team executive. Stallings read the column and the comments, got upset, and announced his plans to resign at the end of the season. Instead, Bill Bidwill fired him on the spot, with several games to go. And with Stallings suddenly available, Alabama hired him. I'm still waiting for my 'Bama championship ring.

Gene Stallings had a remote-control clicker in his right hand, running the play on the large video screen behind his desk, over and over again.

The coach, in a foul mood, was operating some kind of Telestrator from Hell. I'd written about a controversial call that hurt the Cardinals late in their loss at Buffalo the day before. I'd suggested that Stallings was wrong to complain about a late-hit penalty assessed against one of his linebackers. He objected to the opinion and stuck in the game tape, freeze-framing Bills quarterback Jim Kelly and the key moments a jillion times to illustrate his point. What, was this the Zapruder film?

Stallings was exhaling flames. The phone rang in his office. Stallings listened a while, and for the next five minutes lowered his voice to a compassionate whisper.

A stranger had called, long distance: A man who had just fathered a child born with Down syndrome. The new parents were having a difficult time coping with their heartbreak and were given Stallings' number by a mutual friend.

Stallings spoke about his own experience of raising an afflicted child, his son John Mark. Down syndrome occurs when a child is born with an extra chromosome in each cell. Children with the condition are mentally impaired and many develop heart defects.

The Stallings family has cherished every moment spent with John Mark.

"Just remember," Stallings told the man, "that your child has a one-way, express ticket to heaven. The rest of us aren't that lucky. You'll get nothing but unconditional love for as long as he's with you. You'll feel blessed that you have him."

Stallings had transformed himself from maniac coach to kindly hospital minister.

He's a remarkable person. I have little in common with Stallings. Politically, he's somewhere to the right of Jerry Falwell. He's an old-school, cattle-ranching, chicken-fried-southern, military-minded, 57-year-old authority figure. This is one tough hombre. But he also has a heart the size of Paris, Texas, his hometown.

We aren't supposed to lead cheers in the newspaper. Sorry. I'll be screaming at the television set during the Sugar Bowl, hoping that Stallings and his No. 2 Alabama team beat No. 1 Miami for the national championship. I'm happy that he's vindicated himself as a coach. It's time that Stallings got some positive recognition. Until now, he has been a good coach at the wrong place.

Stallings had losing records at Texas A&M and with the St. Louis-Phoenix Cardinals, and was fired at each stop. But he coached the military-school Aggies during the Vietnam era. And his 17-24-1 record with Bill Bidwill's Cardinals doesn't look so awful when we see that the patently aimless Big Red have gone 13-40 since his departure.

Stallings is 30-6 in three years at Alabama, and he has united the Alabama family after years of the infighting that followed the retirement and subsequent death of legendary coach Paul "Bear" Bryant.

"Do I feel vindicated? Not at all," Stallings said. "I feel like I've done a good job wherever I've been. To say I told you so just isn't my style."

What is his style?

He is the tough Texan with a temper that rages like an oil well ablaze. He has a voice so deep and intimidating that it can hush a room full of violent, 250-pound football players. He is so blatantly honest that he once offered to kiss Bidwill's posterior — in exchange for a better long-snapper for field goals.

He is the man who visits hospitals daily. He's arguably the world's greatest dad. He's the coach who has commanded loyalty from a wide spectrum of players — equally adored by urban blacks and strapping farm boys.

Much of who Gene Stallings is can be explained by the presence of John Mark in his life for the last 30 years.

"From my relationship with John Mark, I have learned to listen to my players more," Stallings said. "I want to win every game, but this is a game, not life and death. I've got children of my own. It's not like I haven't been through a crisis from time to time.

"I've learned to be more tolerant of the less gifted. If I see a player who isn't as talented give me everything he's got, I'm going to be on his side. But by the same token, I'm also less tolerant of the gifted who are lazy. If you have God-given talent, there's no excuse not to give your best."

Parents usually shape the character of their children. In the Stallings home, John Mark has shaped the character of his parents and four sisters. John Mark Stallings is their touchstone.

"I've had the best of both worlds," Stallings said. "I've had four daughters and John Mark. I've been able to see my girls grow up, meet nice boys and go through all of their various stages. John Mark has had his accomplishments, too."

When John Mark was born on June 11, 1962, Stallings passed out in the hospital. The doctors told Stallings that the boy wouldn't live five years and recommended that they institutionalize him.

"No, we were going to raise him and be proud of him," Stallings said. "If we were going to a restaurant, John Mark was going. When the girls brought home their dates, we weren't going to hide him. If he wanted to go to practice with me, I put him right next to me on the sideline like any coach would his son. We wanted to make his life as normal as possible."

John Mark made it to 5, and the doctors said he wouldn't make it to 10.

John Mark made it to 10, and the doctors said age 20 was out of the question.

John Mark made it to 20, and the doctors stopped making predictions.

The love of a doting family can be a miracle elixir, stronger and more sustaining than a doctor's curative touch. John Mark is 30 now, and there is a sadness in Stallings' voice when he discusses him.

"John Mark has problems," Stallings said. "He's slowing down. But I try not to think about how much time he has remaining. I just appreciate every day we have together. He does more for us than what we do for him, because he raises our spirits every day.

"It's Christmas time, and every one we spend with John Mark makes it a little bit more special. You know, John still believes in Santa Claus, and he's always the first one down the stairs on Christmas morning."

John Mark believes he's the Alabama team trainer, and one of his new Christmas presents was a kit of medical supplies. "He thinks he has the most important job at Alabama," Stallings said. "I don't rate."

Paper chasing the debate

BERNIE BIT • It was fun to sample the big game of politics during this presidential debate at Washington University. I'm a political junkie, and if I wasn't a sportswriter, I would have probably covered politics — our greatest sport — instead.

The spinning began two hours before the first question was asked of the three candidates for president. The pre-debate spin. A warm-up session for political handlers. Your tax dollars at work. Only in America.

The dueling memoranda started in the afternoon when a Bill Clinton staffer distributed a one-page release, criticizing President Bush on a variety of issues. Ten minutes later, a Bush attaché gave the press corps a two-page counterattack. I don't know where the Ross Perot people were, but the Bush and Clinton campaigns killed enough trees for all three contenders. Most reporters ignored the typed statements. I saw one guy knock over a cup of coffee and clean it up with a Bush release, which contained more paper. A lot of writers used the more efficient Clinton sheet as a dinner placemat.

Hours later, the debate was over. Time to assemble. Packs of emphatic spin doctors moved into the press center, to provide an instant review for the media. That's spinning: a wildly subjective interpretation of how each candidate performed.

It's an art form. A ballet of pandemonium, as spinners bump into reporters, bang into tables, get tangled up in television wires and occasionally spin into one another — while never pausing from their sound bites to take one breath of oxygen.

And yet, this madness is choreographed. Before the debate the Bush campaign issued diagrams showing where "senior spinners" and just plain, old "spinners" should position themselves after the show.

Moments after the debate, Bob Beckel — a Democratic consultant who was a top adviser for Walter Mondale's presidential campaign in 1984 — stood near the back of the press room and watched the spinners whirl into action.

"There are two skills to this," Beckel said. "One is to figure out what the other spinner on the other side is saying first and then try to take away his best arguments.

"In other words, if they say President Bush came across as strong, what you say is 'The most striking thing to me is how weak President Bush came across.' And the most important thing to do: no matter what happens, declare victory."

A reporter approached Beckel, who immediately offered a superb demonstration of the craft. Beckel shook his head. He seemed genuinely saddened for President Bush.

"If you're Bush's people, right now you've got to try and salvage something," Beckel said. "Not that I'm saying Bush did a bad job, but it looked like someone put downers in the guy's milk."

Who won? Well, if you tried to be neutral, it's stretching the imagination to say that anyone dominated.

President Bush seemed stuck on the idea that America isn't too bad off, despite piles of economic data indicating otherwise.

Clinton tried to be all things to all people and offered too many simplistic solutions.

Perot rattled off crackling one-liners — significant if he were running for Jay Leno's job instead of the White House.

But just ask a spinner to declare the winner, and amazing things happen. They'll tell us we didn't really hear what we just heard. They'll swear that the candidate didn't say what he just said.

So let's spin.

"I think Bill Clinton came in a distant third," said Samuel Skinner, the former White House Chief of Staff. "He just didn't rise to the level of the other two."

Bush won, then.

"I'm dumbfounded at Bush's performance," said Sen. Joseph Biden, a Democrat from Delaware. "Bush just took a nail and drove it into his coffin tonight."

Let's spin this way: Did Bush hurt Clinton with the attacks on Clinton's character?

"We made great progress advancing the President's standing," said Charles Black, a Bush senior adviser. "There are many issues of trust and Bill Clinton did not clear up a single one."

And spin . . .

"Just a terrific performance by Bill Clinton," said George Stephanopoulos, Clinton's director of communications. "I give him an A-plus. He answered all the scurrilous, silly patriotism charges once and for all, and showed how George Bush demeans the office."

At one point, White House spokesman Marlin Fitzwater spun into a crowd of reporters standing by Sen. Jay Rockefeller, the Democrat from West Virginia. The two men were so close, you could hear simultaneous spins. Spins in stereo.

Rockefeller in the right ear: "George Bush never looked the American people in the eye. It's a metaphor for his presidency."

Fitzwater in the left ear: "Clinton showed why he's very weak, very naive or very reckless concerning foreign policy."

I'm dizzy.

His way: Barkley is trashing, charming Barcelona

BERNIE BIT • Sir Charles all but organized a nightly street festival in Barcelona, and fans and athletes from around the world followed him on his evening rounds. Barkley isn't for everybody, but I find the guy to be wildly entertaining.

BARCELONA, Spain

He's outrageous, outgoing, outstanding and occasionally out of control. This is how Charles Barkley, the bad boy of Barcelona, is spending his summer vacation.

He has: (1) Mocked Prince Rainier of Monaco; (2) Elbowed a 175-pound Angolan player; (3) Been charged with two technical fouls (4); Hung on the rim after thunder dunks; (4) Taunted the anti-American crowd; (5) Intimidated opponents; (6) Upset his teammates; (7), Filled notebooks with his uncensored quotes; (8) Sparred with the U.S. media; (9) Aggravated the stuffy International Olympic Committee by writing a column for USA Today; (10) Led the Dream Team in scoring.

If Barkley attracted as much defense as controversy, he might not be so dominant in the Olympic basketball games. Barkley, quite simply, has been the USA's most unstoppable player, averaging 22 points through four games, shooting a preposterous 74 percent.

Sure, most of the shots are coming on layups and dunks, but that's because timid players from Angola, Croatia, Germany and Brazil didn't dare go near Barkley. They are terrified of Barkley's 250-pound body, intimidated by his fierce persona. Listed at 6 feet 6 but really about 6-4, he is a raging, burly bull who claims territorial rights to the lane . . . and will enforce them.

Barkley also has been the USA's most unstoppable personality, generating more media attention than perhaps any other athlete here — his photograph and words splattered across newspapers in Spain and Europe, his every action monitored by fans and the press.

"A negative thing about Charles' behavior is that it tends to overshadow his basketball," Magic Johnson said. "People overlook the kind of player he is. He's been sensational. He's calmed down, concentrated on basketball, and it's beautiful to watch."

Everyone — teammates, opponents and the media — has a difficult time understanding the many sides of Charles Barkley, 29. The Philadelphia 76ers stopped trying after last season, when they traded him to Phoenix.

Barkley humorously flaunts his bad manners, as when the Dream Team dined with Prince Rainier while training in Monaco before the Olympics.

"They say we have to stop eating when he stops eating," Barkley said before chowing down. "But what if he's not hungry and just has a snack and I'm starving? Does that mean I have to eat fast?"

For all his fiery antics, Barkley also telephoned a Philadelphia sportswriter (with whom he had feuded) to offer encouragement when the writer spent a long time recovering from surgery. In Philadelphia, Barkley regularly showed up at hospitals unannounced to visit sick children he'd read about.

Pat Williams, an Orlando Magic executive who once served as Sixers GM, described Barkley this way: "Most guys are jerks in private who do things in public that make you think they're nice. Charles is a wonderful guy in private who does things in public that make you think he's a jerk."

Barkley has a theory on the criticism he receives.

"Any time you're a strong black man and have your own individualistic standards, they're going to get you," he said this week. "That's the way of the society we live in."

It was pointed out that he has teammates who are strong and black — and that they had admonished him for elbowing the skinny Angolan.

"No," Barkley said. "They're different from me. They're not going to say the things that should be said. Michael Jordan says that I say the things they want to say. But they won't say them. That's why they're different."

Barkley, who has a deal with Nike, has indicated that he will ignore the U.S. Olympic Committee policy that the Dream Teamers must wear Reebok-made warmups during the medal ceremony.

"There are only three things in life that I have to do," Barkley said. "I have to stay black, I have to pay taxes, and I have to die. Other than that, don't tell me what I have to do."

Barkley halfheartedly protests his treatment in the media. He seems to forget that he initiates the furor with actions and comments.

Inside, he's loving every minute of it. For he — and not Michael Jordan — is the U.S. player drawing the most response from the animated crowds at Palau D'Esports de Badalona.

"This is a great way to spend your summer, and this has been a great month for me," Barkley said. "This has probably been the best month of my life — the trade and this basketball team here."

And he will not apologize for anything — the blowout victories, his unruly behavior, the Ugly American image.

"We came here to do a job," Barkley said. "We're here to tell these other teams that they've been holding the gold medal for four years, and that's long enough. We've come to take it back home."

By the time Barkley goes home, Barcelona may never be the same.

Bosnian runner embodies struggle to win freedom

BERNIE BIT • There are times when I hear a baseball or football player talk about how they overcame the adversity of a sore knee, a wet field, or a delayed charter flight, and I just laugh inside. Read this story of one Olympic runner's extreme determination, and you'll understand why.

BARCELONA, Spain

Each day, she would say a prayer as she laced her shoes, hoping the sniper fire would miss her. Then she would wait until she heard the wail of the sirens, and that was the signal for Mirsada Buric to slip out onto the streets of Sarajevo to begin her training run.

"You never knew when a grenade would come down or someone would shoot," said Buric, a 22-year-old distance runner from Bosnia. "We had a stadium, but I could not train there. It was bombed out. The streets were the best place. The streets were empty during the air-raid alerts. It was easier to move around that way, to avoid danger."

Buric stayed close to the walls, which provided cover. When the volley of bullets intensified, she'd sneak into a doorway or scoot between buildings. As she jogged past the row houses, she could hear her fellow Bosnians shout words of encouragement through the windows of their basements. And this energized her.

"My people gave me tremendous strength," Buric said. "I could hear them talk to me, and I knew I was not running for myself but for them as well. Their cheers became my resistance against the shooting."

Buric outran the bullets. She outran them all the way to the Olympic Games, where she'll represent Bosnia in the women's 3,000-meter run. But Buric represents something far more profound: the almighty power of a spirit that demands nothing less than complete liberty.

"Things are very bad at home," Buric said in an interview at the athletes' village. "Our people do not eat enough. And winter is near. Then it will be worse. But we must go on to fight for our freedom."

There is no story at the 1992 Summer Olympics as extraordinary as Buric's. There are more famous athletes, those who have more money and commercial contracts and no problems. You know, such as preening track star Carl Lewis, so self-important that he marches during the opening ceremony with a cellular telephone in his hand, making calls.

No one has endured more misery to get here than Buric. The world must find out about Buric, who symbolizes a lost Olympic purity that never can be bought, sold or traded. She is the flame of these Olympic Games.

Buric's ordeal along the journey to Barcelona is inspirational, because it reveals the triumph of internal will over external forces. The world needs to know how she survived the bombings and atrocities that crushed her village, killed her friends, terrorized her family, held her hostage, took away her running shoes and just about everything else but her desire.

And the world needs to know more about Sarajevo, Bosnia's capital. For the last five months the city has been the bull's eye of relentless Serbian assaults during an excruciating civil war that has shattered Yugoslavia. And Buric, so good and thoughtful with words — she is a graduate of a journalism school in Sarajevo — can tell us the story.

"The Olympics are important to me, for I think it is the greatest honor to represent a newly independent country that is struggling to survive," Buric said. "Perhaps, through me, others will learn about the resiliency of our people."

In June, Buric was held prisoner by Serbian forces for 13 days, along with her family and 350 other Muslims. Released, she was left homeless in the weeks leading into Barcelona, living in the shell of the battered Sarajevo Holiday Inn. Much of the sixth and seventh floors were destroyed, but Buric's sixth-floor room remained solid.

Buric already has lost an uncle, and her younger brother is missing and presumed dead. Both were victims of a Serbian attack, taken from the army barracks near town.

"Physically, I am here in Spain," Buric said. "But my heart, it is in Sarajevo. I always think of my people. My brother. My friends. Always. It is very quiet here, and I can train in the Olympic Stadium, which is beautiful. But I don't sleep any better. I think about my home.

"I enjoy the Olympic Village, but it also saddens me. It's very difficult to have a pleasant life for these two weeks when I know that friends and family members and the lost souls are suffering back home."

Buric said she nearly was shot twice by snipers, and once a grenade exploded less than a block away from her. But she continued to train, always changing her route to avoid any pattern making her more identifiable to the snipers.

Buric's most terrifying brush with death came during a bombardment that lasted nearly three days. She crawled into a basement as the mortar shells pounded the village. When Buric and her neighbors were taken into custody by Serbian troops and held for 13 days, she attempted to stay in shape by running in place, skipping and climbing steps.

In the end, Buric and the others were released in exchange for 38 Serbian soldiers. But all of her gear was confiscated by the soldiers. Buric had to borrow shoes to continue roadwork and still hasn't found a comfortable pair. Despite her firm determination, Buric isn't in peak condition. She is a long shot for a medal.

Still, she never stopped running. Her city was being choked by bombs and bullets, but she found the oxygen. A war could not keep her from these Olympic Games.

"The only way to remain sane is to try to maintain a normal routine," Buric said. "You conclude that there is no other way. You just do what is necessary to survive each hour and each day. I just wish I could see the day when the fighting will stop."

As late as last week, there were no assurances that Buric would make it here. Serbs had the Sarajevo airport sealed off. But Buric and four teammates were taken to the airport in armored trucks. And they arrived in Barcelona on Saturday, just three hours before the opening ceremony.

"Even when the plane left the runway, I could not believe we would make it," Buric said.

When the Bosnian team marched into the Olympic Stadium, the crowd of 65,000 responded warmly. Each section of the stadium stood and waved and cheered as the small delegation passed by.

"The people were standing for us," Buric said. "I had tears."

Buric flinched later in the ceremony, when fireworks exploded to end the opening-night celebration.

"The noise," Buric said, "was just like the shooting at home."

More tears, these for Sarajevo.

Quake perspective: Thankful for warm soda, crackers

BERNIE BIT • The editors back in St. Louis didn't care about the difficult circumstances caused by the earthquake that interrupted the World Series. I had to get the story in. That was my assignment, and deadline was fast approaching. A man's gotta do what he's gotta do …

SAN FRANCISCO

So you want to be a sportswriter. Glamorous job. Expense accounts, going to games for free, rubbing elbows with famous stars and athletes. Won't you join me? I am writing this at 7:30 Thursday evening. I am on the 12th floor, the top floor, of a downtown hotel. I just felt the building shake. Another aftershock.

The first happened in the wee hours of Thursday morning and rocked me out of a sound sleep. I rolled over. I went back to sleep. The earth moves; I snore.

When the building gyrated just now, I did not flinch. I shrugged and kept banging the keys of the word processor. This one was a 4.3 on the Richter scale. I don't pay attention to anything under 5.0. I am becoming wacky, like a real Californian. I am becoming oblivious to earthquakes.

I am also becoming a vagrant. Because of the Tuesday Quake, it has been three days since my last shower. It has been three days since my last hot meal. When I walk on the streets, strangers get a whiff of me and offer me quarters.

Only Thursday morning did the hotel regain electricity, meaning that I spent the last two nights in darkness. Using a candle to find my way, I'd walk up 11 flights of stairs and find my room. I tripped once. The couple I nearly bowled over were nice about it.

No standard food was available, so I raided the mini-refrigerator in my room. Tuesday night, dinner was two warm beers, a pack of sesame-seed crackers, a can of Hawaiian potato chips and a small box of cookies. Wednesday night, dinner was warm orange juice, warm club soda, a bag of sourdough crackers and a candy bar.

By the way, boss, that comes to about $326.89 on the hotel bill. What, you've never had a $14 orange juice? Oh, no wonder those mini-bars are so convenient.

Trust me, I'm not really complaining. It's easy to be grouchy, up until the time you visit Oakland and see cars crushed by a collapsed freeway. It makes you thankful for those warm sodas and crackers.

You still want to be a sportswriter? OK. Come back with me to Tuesday night at Candlestick Park, when the earthquake hit the Bay Area.

After saying a prayer, I headed down to interview players and officials about the earthquake.

By the time I came back to the press box, cops were clearing out the stadium, and they refused to let us write stories or use the telephone. I was required to file a story and had about 90 minutes until deadline. There was no way I could get out of the gridlocked parking lot and back downtown in time.

Simple. I put fresh batteries in the computer and headed to my rental car. I turned on the interior lights and placed the computer on the steering wheel. I tapped out what I had just witnessed.

I had only 30 minutes to get the story in. What now?

No sweat. There's a neighborhood next to Candlestick, a neighborhood that is one of the worst in San Francisco. But it was also a neighborhood that had telephones.

I slowed down at the entrance of the housing project. A gentleman waved a baseball bat at me, and threatened me to keep out unless I wanted trouble.

Of course, I had a rational response:

"I will pay you money, a large amount of money, to let me use your phone," I said.

"That will be $40," he said. Deal. He became my bodyguard as we drove through the streets of the project, which was unlit.

I got out of the car, and my guardian waved off would-be predators. He marched me to an apartment. I asked a young woman about the phone.

"I want $40," she said.

Let's go to the calculator: That's $80 for one phone call, one story. But it was an important story. Deal.

As I hooked the computer to the phone to transmit the story, the apartment occupants were in the kitchen, smoking a substance in a pipe.

Hint: It wasn't Prince Albert.

They asked me if I wanted some. I said no, but I'd be happy to have a nice, cold Budweiser. Unless it cost $40. They gave me one on the house.

It made a man proud to be a sportswriter.

PHOTO CREDITS

Post-Dispatch Photographers

Jarrett Baker • 11

Douglas Clifford • 117

Robert Cohen • 33, 132

Wayne Crosslin • 52

Andrew Cutraro • 57, 80

Scott Dine • 140

Wendi Fitzgerald • 158, 172

J.B. Forbes • 28, 84, 146

Chris Lee • 12, 24, 29, 40, 48, 49, 92, 112, 120, 124, 125, 148, 149, 189

Huy Richard Mach • 36

Kevin Manning • 69, 77, 78, 100, 203, 209

Odell Mitchell Jr. • 68, 73, 136

Post-Dispatch Files • 7, 143, 181, 200

Jerry Naunheim Jr. • 60

Laurie Skrivan • 15, 20, 44, 96, 105

Larry Williams • 53

Other Photographers

Eric Draper, Associated Press • 178

Cover

Jerry Naunheim Jr. • Chris Lee • Laurie Skrivan • Dilip Vishwanat

Back Cover

Gabriel B. Tait